BERNAL DÍAZ

THE BETRAYAL OF MONTEZUMA

TRANSLATED BY J. M. COHEN

PENGUIN BOOKS

PENGUIN BOOKS

Published by the Penguin Group
Penguin Books Ltd, 27 Wrights Lane, London W8 5TZ, England
Penguin Books USA Inc., 375 Hudson Street, New York, New York 10014, USA
Penguin Books Australia Ltd, Ringwood, Victoria, Australia
Penguin Books Canada Ltd, 10 Alcorn Avenue, Toronto, Ontario, Canada M4V 3B2
Penguin Books (NZ) Ltd, 182–190 Wairau Road, Auckland 10, New Zealand

Penguin Books Ltd, Registered Offices: Harmondsworth, Middlesex, England

This selection is from J. M. Cohen's translation of
The Conquest of New Spain, published in Penguin Classics 1963
This edition published 1995
1 3 5 7 9 10 8 6 4 2

Printed in England by Clays Ltd, St Ives plc

We left Iztapalapa with a large escort of these great *Caciques*, and followed the causeway, which is eight yards wide and goes straight to the city of Mexico that I do not think it curves at all. Wide though it was, it was so crowded with people that there was hardly room for them all. Some were going to Mexico and others coming away, besides those who had come out to see us, and we could hardly get through the crowds that were there. For the towers and the *cues* were full, and they came in canoes from all parts of the lake. No wonder, since they had never seen horses or men like us before!

With such wonderful sights to gaze on we did not know what to say, or if this was real that we saw before our eyes. On the land side there were great cities, and on the lake many more. The lake was crowded with canoes. At intervals along the causeway there were many bridges, and before us was the great city of Mexico. As for us, we were scarcely four hundred strong, and we well remembered the words and warnings of the people of Huexotzinco and Tlascala and Tlamanalco, and the many other warnings we had received to beware of entering the city of Mexico, since they would kill us as soon as they had us inside. Let the interested reader consider whether there is not much to ponder in this narrative of mine. What men in all the world have shown such daring? But let us go on.

We marched along our causeway to a point where another small causeway branches off to another city called Coyoacan, and there, beside some towerlike buildings, which were their shrines, we were met by many more *Caciques* and dignitaries in very rich cloaks. The different chieftains wore different brilliant liveries, and the causeways were full of them. Montezuma had sent these great *Caciques* in advance to receive us, and as soon as they came before Cortes they told him in their language that we were welcome, and as a sign of peace they touched the ground with their hands and kissed it.

There we halted for some time while Cacamatzin, the lord of Texcoco, and the lords of Iztapalapa, Tacuba, and Coyoacan went ahead to meet the great Montezuma, who approached in a rich litter, accompanied by other great lords and feudal *Caciques* who owned vassals. When we came near to Mexico, at a place where there were some other small towers, the great Montezuma descended from his litter, and these other great *Caciques* supported him beneath a marvellously rich canopy of green feathers, decorated with gold work, silver, pearls, and *chalchihuites*, which hung from a sort of border. It was a marvellous sight. The great Montezuma was magnificently clad, in their fashion, and wore sandals of a kind for which their name is *cotaras*, the soles of which are of gold and the upper parts ornamented with precious stones. And the four lords who supported him were richly clad also in garments that seem to have been kept ready for them on the road so that they could accompany their master. For they had not worn clothes like this when they came out to receive us. There were four other great *Caciques* who carried the canopy above their heads, and many more lords who walked before the great Montezuma, sweeping the ground on which he was to tread, and laying down cloaks so that his feet should not touch the earth. Not one of these chieftains dared to look him in the face. All kept their eyes lowered most reverently except those four lords, his nephews, who were supporting him.

When Cortes saw, heard, and was told that the great Montezuma was approaching, he dismounted from his horse, and when he came near to Montezuma each bowed deeply to the other. Montezuma welcomed our Captain, and Cortes, speaking through Doña Marina, answered by wishing him very good health. Cortes, I think, offered Montezuma his right hand, but Montezuma refused it and extended his own. Then Cortes brought out a necklace which he had been holding. It was made of those elaborately worked and coloured glass beads called *margaritas*, of which I have spoken, and was strung on a gold cord and dipped in musk to give it a good odour. This he hung round the great Montezuma's neck, and as he did so attempted to embrace him. But the great princes who stood round Montezuma grasped Cortes' arm to prevent him, for they considered this an indignity.

Then Cortes told Montezuma that it rejoiced his heart to have seen such a great prince, and that he took his coming in person to receive him and the repeated favours he had done him as a high honour. After this Montezuma made him another complimentary speech, and ordered two of his nephews who were supporting him, the lords of Texcoco and Coyoacan, to go with us and show us our quarters. Montezuma returned to the city with the other two kinsmen of his escort, the lords of Cuitlahuac and Tacuba; and all those grand companies of *Caciques* and dignitaries who had come with him returned also in his train. And as they accompanied their lord we observed them marching with their eyes downcast so that they should not see him, keeping close to the wall as they followed him with great reverence. Thus space was made for us to enter the streets of Mexico without being pressed by the crowd.

Who could now count the multitude of men, women, and boys in the streets, on the roof-tops and in canoes on the waterways, who had come out to see us? It was a wonderful sight and, as I write, it all comes before my eyes as if it had happened only yesterday.

They led us to our quarters, which were in some large houses capable of accommodating us all and had formerly belonged to the great Montezuma's father, who was called Axayacatl. Here Montezuma now kept the great shrines of his gods, and a secret chamber containing gold bars and jewels. This was the treasure he had inherited from his father, which he never touched. Perhaps their reason for lodging us here was that, since they called us *Teules* and considered us as such, they wished to have us near their idols. In any case they took us to this place, where there were many great halls, and a dais hung with the cloth of their country for our Captain, and matting beds with canopies over them for each of us.

On our arrival we entered the large court, where the great Montezuma was awaiting our Captain. Taking him by the hand, the prince led him to his apartment in the hall where he was to lodge, which was very richly furnished in their manner. Montezuma had ready for him a very rich necklace, made of golden crabs, a marvellous piece of work, which he hung round Cortes' neck. His captains were greatly astonished at this sign of honour.

After this ceremony, for which Cortes thanked him through our interpreters, Montezuma said: 'Malinche, you and your brothers are in your own house. Rest awhile.' He then returned to his palace, which was not far off.

We divided our lodgings by companies, and placed our artillery in a convenient spot. Then the order we were to keep was clearly explained to us, and we were warned to be very much on the alert, both the horsemen and the rest of us soldiers. We then ate a sumptuous dinner which they had prepared for us in their native style.

So, with luck on our side, we boldly entered the city of Tenochtitlan or Mexico on 8 November in the year of our Lord 1519.

When the great Montezuma had dined and was told that our Captain and all of us had finished our meal some time ago, he came to our quarters in the grandest state with a great number of princes, all of them his kinsmen. On being told of his approach, Cortes came into the middle of the hall to receive him. Montezuma then took him by the hand, and they brought chairs made in their fashion and very richly decorated in various ways with gold. Montezuma requested our Captain to sit down, and both of them sat, each on his own chair.

Then Montezuma began a very good speech, saying that he was delighted to have such valiant gentlemen as Cortes and the rest of us in his house and his kingdom. That two years ago he had received news of a Captain who had come to Champoton, and that last year also he had received a report of another Captain who had come with four ships. Each time he had wished to see them, and now that he had us with him he was not only at our service but would share all that he possessed with us. He ended by saying that we must truly be the men about whom his ancestors had long ago prophesied, saying that they would come from the direction of the sunrise to rule over these lands, and that he was confirmed in this belief by the valour with which we had fought at Champoton and Tabasco and against the Tlascalans, for lifelike pictures of these battles had been brought to him.

Cortes replied through our interpreters that we did not know how to repay the daily favours we received from him, and that indeed we did come from the direction of the sunrise, and were vassals and servants of a great king called the Emperor Charles, who was ruler over many great princes. Having heard news of Montezuma and what a great prince he was, the Emperor, he said, had sent us to this country to visit him, and to beg them to become Christians, like our Emperor and all of us, so that his soul and those of all his vassals might be saved. Cortes promised to explain to him later how this could be, and how we worship the one true God and who He is, also many other good things which he had already communicated to his ambassadors Tendile, Pitalpitoque, and Quintalbor.

The great Montezuma had some fine gold jewels of various shapes in readiness which he gave to Cortes after this conversation. And to each of our captains he presented small gold objects and three loads of cloaks of rich feather work; and to us soldiers he gave two loads of cloaks each, all with a princely air. For in every way he was like a great prince. After the distribution of presents, he asked Cortes if we were all brothers and vassals of our great Emperor; and Cortes answered that we were brothers in love and friendship, persons of great distinction, and servants of our great king and lord. Further polite speeches passed between Montezuma and Cortes, but as this was the first time he had visited us and we did not want to tire him, the conversation ended.

Montezuma had ordered his stewards to provide us with everything we needed for our way of living: maize, grindstones, women to make our bread, fowls, fruit, and plenty of fodder for the horses. He then took leave of us all with the greatest courtesy, and we accompanied him to the street. However, Cortes ordered us not to go far from our quarters for the present until we knew better what conduct to observe.

Next day Cortes decided to go to Montezuma's palace. But first he sent to know whether the prince was busy and to inform him of our coming. He took four captains with him: Pedro de Alvarado, Juan Velazquez de Leon, Diego de Ordaz, and Gonzalo de Sandoval, and five of us soldiers.

When Montezuma was informed of our coming, he advanced into the middle of the hall to receive us, closely surrounded by his nephews, for no other chiefs were allowed to enter his palace or communicate with him except upon important business. Cortes and Montezuma exchanged bows, and clasped hands. Then Montezuma led Cortes to his own dais, and setting him down on his right, called for more seats, on which he ordered us all to sit also.

Cortes began to make a speech through our interpreters, saying that we were all now rested, and that in coming to see and speak with such a great prince we had fulfilled the purpose of our voyage and the orders of our lord the King. The principal things he had come to say on behalf of our Lord God had already been communicated to Montezuma through his three ambassadors, on that occasion in the sandhills when he did us the favour of sending us the golden moon and sun. We had then told him that we were Christians and worshipped one God alone, named Jesus Christ, who had suffered His passion and death to save us; and that what they worshipped as gods were not gods but devils, which were evil things, and if they were ugly to look at, their deeds were uglier. But he had proved to them how evil and ineffectual their gods were, as both the prince and his people would observe in the course of time, since, where we had put up crosses such as their ambassadors had seen, they had been too frightened to appear before them.

The favour he now begged of the great Montezuma was that he should listen to the words he now wished to speak. Then he very carefully expounded the creation of the world, how we are all brothers, the children of one mother and father called Adam and Eve; and how such a brother as our great Emperor, grieving for the perdition of so many souls as their idols were leading to hell, where they burnt in living flame, had sent us to tell him this, so that he might put a stop to it, and so that they might give up the worship of idols and make no more human sacrifices—for all men are brothers—and commit no more robbery or sodomy. He also promised that in the course of time the King would send some men who lead holy lives among us, much better than our own, to explain this more fully, for we had only come to give them warning. Therefore he begged Montezuma to do as he was asked.

As Montezuma seemed about to reply, Cortes broke off his speech, saying to those of us who were with him: 'Since this is only the first attempt, we have now done our duty.'

'My lord Malinche,' Montezuma replied, 'these arguments of yours have been familiar to me for some time. I understand what you said to my ambassadors on the sandhills about the three gods and the cross, also what you preached in the various towns through which you passed. We have given you no answer, since we have worshipped our own gods here from the beginning and know them to be good. No doubt yours are good also, but do not trouble to tell us any more about them at present. Regarding the creation of the world, we have held the same belief for many ages, and for this reason we are certain that you are those who our ancestors predicted would come from the direction of the sunrise. As for your great King, I am in his debt and will give him of what I possess. For, as I have already said, two years ago I had news of the Captains who came in ships, by the road that you came, and said they were servants of this great king of yours. I should like to know if you are all the same people.'

Cortes answered that we were all brothers and servants of the Emperor, and that they had come to discover a route and explore the seas and ports, so that when they knew them well we could follow, as we had done. Montezuma was referring to the expeditions of Francisco Hernadez de Cordoba and of Grijalva, the first voyages of discovery. He said that ever since that time he had wanted to invite some of these men to visit the cities of his kingdom, where he would receive them and do them honour, and that now his gods had fulfilled his desire, for we were in his house, which we might call our own. Here we might rest and enjoy ourselves, for we should receive good treatment. If on other occasions he had sent to forbid our entrance into his city, it was not of his own free will, but because his vassals were afraid. For they told him we shot out flashes of lightning, and killed many Indians with our horses, and that we were angry *Teules*, and other such childish stories. But now that he had seen us, he knew that we were of flesh and blood and very intelligent, also very brave. Therefore he had a far greater esteem for us than these reports had given him, and would share with us what he had.

We all thanked him heartily for his signal good will, and Montezuma replied with a laugh, because in his princely manner he spoke very gaily: 'Malinche, I know that these people of Tlascala with whom you are so friendly have told you that I am a sort of god or *Teule*, and keep nothing in any of my houses that is not made of silver and gold and precious stones. But I know very well that you are too intelligent to believe this and will take it as a joke. See now, Malinche, my body is made of flesh and blood like yours, and my houses and palaces are of stone, wood, and plaster. It is true that I am a great king, and have inherited the riches of my ancestors, but the lies and nonsense you have heard of us are not true. You must take them as a joke, as I take the story of your thunders and lightnings.'

Cortes answered also with a laugh that enemies always speak evil and tell lies about the people they hate, but he knew he could not hope to find a more magnificent prince in that land, and there was good reason why his fame should have reached our Emperor.

While this conversation was going on, Montezuma quietly sent one of his nephews, a great *Cacique*, to order his stewards to bring certain pieces of gold, which had apparently been set aside as a gift for Cortes, and ten loads of fine cloaks which he divided: the gold and cloaks between Cortes and the four captains, and for each of us soldiers two gold necklaces, each worth ten pesos, and two loads of cloaks. The gold that he then gave us was worth in all more than a thousand pesos, and he gave it all cheerfully, like a great and valiant prince.

As it was now past midday and he did not wish to be importunate, Cortes said to Montezuma: 'My lord, the favours you do us increase, load by load, every day, and it is now the hour of your dinner.' Montezuma answered that he thanked us for visiting him. We then took our leave with the greatest courtesy, and returned to our quarters, talking as we went of the prince's fine breeding and manners and deciding to show him the greatest respect in every way, and to remove our quilted caps in his presence, which we always did.

The great Montezuma was about forty years old, of good height, well proportioned, spare and slight, and not very dark, though of the usual Indian complexion. He did not wear his hair long but just over his ears, and he had a short black beard, well-shaped and thin. His face was rather long and cheerful, he had fine eyes, and in his appearance and manner could express geniality or, when necessary, a serious composure. He was very neat and clean, and took a bath every afternoon. He had many women as his mistresses, the daughters of chieftains, but two legitimate wives who were *Caciques* in their own right, and when he had intercourse with any of them it was so secret that only some of his servants knew of it. He was quite free from sodomy. The clothes he wore one day he did not wear again till three or four days later. He had a guard of two hundred chieftains lodged in rooms beside his own, only some of whom were permitted to speak to him. When they entered his presence they were compelled to take off their rich cloaks and put on others of little value. They had to be clean and walk barefoot, with their eyes downcast, for they were not allowed to look him in the face, and as they approached they had to make three obeisances, saying as they did so, "Lord, my lord, my great lord!' Then, when they had said what they had come to say, he would dismiss them with a few words. They did not turn their backs on him as they went out, only turning round when they had left the room. Another thing I noticed was that when other great chiefs came from distant lands about disputes or on business, they too had to take off their shoes and put on poor cloaks before entering Montezuma's apartments; and they were not allowed to enter the palace immediately but had to linger for a while near the door, since to enter hurriedly was considered disrespectful.

For each meal his servants prepared him more than thirty dishes cooked in their native style, which they put over small earthenware braziers to prevent them from getting cold. They cooked more than three hundred plates of food the great Montezuma was going to eat, and more than a thousand more for the guard. I have heard that they used to cook him the flesh of young boys. But as he had such a variety of dishes, made of so many different ingredients, we could not tell whether a dish was of human flesh or anything else, since every day they cooked fowls, turkeys, pheasants, local partridges, quail, tame and wild duck, venison, wild boar, marsh birds, pigeons, hares and rabbits, also many other kinds of birds and beasts native to their country, so numerous that I cannot quickly name them all. I know for certain, however, that after our Captain spoke against the sacrifice of human beings and the eating of their flesh, Montezuma ordered that it should no longer be served to him.

Let us now turn to the way his meals were served, which was like this. If it was cold, they built a large fire of live coals made by burning the bark of a tree which gave off no smoke. The smell of the bark from which they made these coals was very sweet. In order that he should get no more heat than he wanted, they placed a sort of screen in front of it adorned with the figures of idols worked in gold. He would sit on a soft low stool, which was richly worked. His table, which was also low and decorated in the same way, was covered with white tablecloths and rather long napkins of the same material. Then four very clean and beautiful girls brought water for his hands in one of those basins that they call *xicales*. They held others like plates beneath it to catch the water, and brought him towels. Two other women brought him maize-cakes.

When he began his meal they placed in front of him a sort of wooden screen, richly decorated with gold, so that no one should see him eat. Then the four women retired, and four great chieftains, all old men, stood beside him. He talked with them every now and then and asked them questions, and as a great favour he would sometimes offer one of them a dish of whatever tasted best. They say that these were his closest relations and advisers and judges of lawsuits, and if he gave them anything to eat they ate it standing, with deep reverence and without looking in his face.

Montezuma's food was served on Cholula ware, some red and some black. While he was dining, the guards in the adjoining rooms did not dare to speak or make a noise above a whisper. His servants brought him some of every kind of fruit that grew in the country, but he ate very little of it. Sometimes they brought him in cups of pure gold a drink made from the cocoaplant, which they said he took before visiting his wives. We did not take much notice of this at the time, though I saw them bring in a good fifty large jugs of this chocolate, all frothed up, of which he would drink a little. They always served it with great reverence. Sometimes some little humpbacked dwarfs would be present at his meals, whose bodies seemed almost to be broken in the middle. These were his jesters. There were other Indians who told him jokes and must have been his clowns, and others who sang and danced, for Montezuma was very fond of music and entertainment and would reward his entertainers with the leavings of the food and chocolate. The same four women removed the tablecloths and again most reverently brought him water for his hands. Then Montezuma would talk to these four old chieftains about matters that interested him, and they would take their leave with great ceremony. He stayed behind to rest.

As soon as the great Montezuma had dined, all the guards and many more of his household servants ate in their turn. I think more than a thousand plates of food must have been brought in for them, and more than two thousand jugs of chocolate frothed up in the Mexican style, and infinite quantities of fruit, so that with his women and serving-maids and bread-makers and chocolate-makers his expenses must have been considerable.

One thing I had forgotten to say is that two more very handsome women served Montezuma when he was at table with maize-cakes kneaded with eggs and other nourishing ingredients. These maize-cakes were very white, and were brought in on plates covered with clean napkins. They brought him a different kind of bread also, in a long ball kneaded with other kinds of nourishing food, and *pachol* cake, as they call it in that country, which is a kind of wafer. They also placed on the table three tubes, much painted and gilded, in which they put liquidamber mixed with some herbs which are called tobacco. When Montezuma had finished his dinner, and the singing and dancing were over and the cloths had been removed, he would inhale the smoke from one of these tubes. He took very little of it, and then fell asleep.

I remember that at that time his steward was a great *Cacique* whom we nicknamed Tapia, and he kept an account of all the revenue that was brought to Montezuma in his books, which were made of paper—their name for which is *amal*—and he had a great house full of these books. But they have nothing to do with our story.

Montezuma had two houses stocked with every sort of

weapon; many of them were richly adorned with gold and precious stones. There were shields large and small, and a sort of broadsword, and two-handed swords set with flint blades that cut much better than our swords, and lances longer than ours, with five-foot blades consisting of many knives. Even when these are driven at a buckler or a shield they are not deflected. In fact they cut like razors, and the Indians can shave their heads with them. They had very good bows and arrows, and double and single-pointed javelins as well as their throwing-sticks and many slings and round stones shaped by hand, and another sort of shield that can be rolled up when they are not fighting, so that it does not get in the way, but which can be opened when they need it in battle and covers their bodies from head to foot. There was also a great deal of cotton armour richly worked on the outside with different coloured feathers, which they used as devices and distinguishing marks, and they had casques and helmets made of wood and bone which were also highly decorated with feathers on the outside. They had other arms of different kinds which I will not mention through fear of prolixity, and workmen skilled in the manufacture of such things, and stewards who were in charge of these arms.

Let us pass on to the aviary. I cannot possibly enumerate every kind of bird that was in it or describe its characteristics. There was everything from the royal eagle, smaller kinds of eagles, and other large birds, down to multi-coloured little birds, and those from which they take the fine green feathers they use in their feather-work. These last birds are about the size of our magpies, and here they are called *quetzals*. There were other birds too which have feathers of five colours: green, red, white, yellow, and blue, but I do not know what they are called. Then there were parrots with different coloured plumage, so many of them that I have forgotten their names. There were also beautifully marked ducks, and bigger ones like them. At the proper season they plucked the feathers of all these birds, which then grew again. All of them were bred in this aviary, and at hatching time the men and women who looked after them would place them on their eggs and clean their nests and feed them, giving each breed of birds its proper food.

In the aviary there was a large tank of fresh water, and in it was another type of bird on long stilt-like legs with a red body, wings, and tail. I do not know its name, but in Cuba birds rather like them are called *ypiris*. Also in this tank there were many other kinds of water birds.

Let us go to another large house where they kept many idols whom they called their fierce gods, and with them all kinds of beasts of prey, tigers and two sorts of lion, and beasts rather like wolves which they call *adives*, and foxes and other small animals, all of them carnivores, and most of them bred there. They were fed on deer, fowls, little dogs, and other creatures which they hunt and also on the bodies of the Indians they sacrificed, as I was told.

I have already described the manner of their sacrifices.

They strike open the wretched Indian's chest with flint knives and hastily tear out the palpitating heart which, with the blood, they present to the idols in whose name they have performed the sacrifice. Then they cut off the arms, thighs, and head, eating the arms and thighs at their ceremonial banquets. The head they hang up on a beam, and the body of the sacrificed man is not eaten but given to the beasts of prey. They also had many vipers in this accursed house, and poisonous snakes which have something that sounds like a bell in their tails. These, which are the deadliest snakes of all, they kept in jars and great pottery vessels full of feathers, in which they laid their eggs and reared their young. They were fed on the bodies of sacrificed Indians and the flesh of dogs that they bred. We know for certain, too, that when they drove us out of Mexico and killed over eight hundred and fifty of our soldiers, they fed those beasts and snakes on their bodies for many days, as I shall relate in due course. These snakes and wild beasts were dedicated to their fierce idols, and kept them company. As for the horrible noise when the lions and tigers roared, and the jackals and foxes howled, and the serpents hissed, it was so appalling that one seemed to be in hell.

I must now speak of the skilled workmen whom Montezuma employed in all the crafts they practised, beginning with the jewellers and workers in silver and gold and various kinds of hollowed objects, which excited the admiration of our great silversmiths at home. Many of the best of them lived in a town called Atzcapotzalco, three miles from Mexico. There were other skilled craftsmen who worked with precious stones and *chalchihuites*, and specialists in feather-work, and very fine painters and carvers. We can form some judgement of what they did then from what we can see of their work today. There are three Indians now living in the city of Mexico, named Marcos de Aquino, Juan de la Cruz, and El Crespillo, who are such magnificent painters and carvers that, had they lived in the age of the Apelles of old, or of Michael Angelo, or Berruguete in our own day, they would be counted in the same rank.

Let us go on to the women, the weavers and sempstresses, who made such a huge quantity of fine robes with very elaborate feather designs. These things were generally brought from some towns in the province of Cotaxtla, which is on the north coast, quite near San Juan de Ulua. In Montezuma's own palaces very fine cloths were woven by those chieftains' daughters whom he kept as mistresses; and the daughters of other dignitaries, who lived in a kind of retirement like nuns in some houses close to the great *cue* of Huichilobos, wore robes entirely of feather-work. Out of devotion for that god and a female deity who was said to preside over marriage, their fathers would place them in religious retirement until they found husbands. They would then take them out to be married.

Now to speak of the great number of performers whom

Montezuma kept to entertain him. There were dancers and stilt-walkers, and some who seemed to fly as they leapt through the air, and men rather like clowns to make him laugh. There was a whole quarter full of these people who had no other occupation. He had as many workmen as he needed, too, stone-cutters, masons, and carpenters, to keep his house in repair.

We must not forget the gardens with their many varieties of flowers and sweet-scented trees planted in order, and their ponds and tanks of fresh water into which a stream flowed at one end and out of which it flowed at the other, and the baths he had there, and the variety of small birds that nested in the branches, and the medicinal and useful herbs that grew there. His gardens were a wonderful sight, and required many gardeners to take care of them. Everything was built of stone and plaster; baths and walks and closets and rooms like summerhouses where they danced and sang. There was so much to see in these gardens, as everywhere else, that we could not tire of contemplating his great riches and the large number of skilled Indians employed in the many crafts they practised.

When we had already been in Mexico for four days, and neither our Captain nor anyone else had left our quarters except to visit these houses and gardens, Cortes said it would be a good thing to visit the large square of Tlatelolco and see the great *cue* of Huichilobos. So he sent Aguilar, Doña Marina, and his own young page Orteguilla, who by now knew something of the language, to ask for Montezuma's approval of this plan. On receiving his request, the prince replied that we were welcome to go, but for fear that we might offer some offence to his idols he would himself accompany us with many of his chieftains. Leaving the palace in his fine litter, when he had gone about half way, he dismounted beside some shrines, since he considered it an insult to his gods to visit their dwelling in a litter. Some of the great chieftains then supported him by the arms, and his principal vassals walked before him, carrying two staves, like sceptres raised on high as a sign that the great Montezuma was approaching. When riding in his litter he had carried a rod, partly of gold and partly of wood, held up like a wand of justice. The prince now climbed the steps of the great *cue*, escorted by many *papas*, and began to burn incense and perform other ceremonies for Huichilobos.

Let us leave Montezuma, who had gone ahead as I have said, and return to Cortes and our soldiers. We carried our weapons as was our custom, both by night and day. Indeed, Montezuma was so used to our visiting him armed that he did not think it strange. I say this because our Captain and those of us who had horses went to Tlatelolco mounted, and the majority of our men were fully equipped. On reaching the market-place, escorted by the many *Caciques* whom Montezuma had assigned to us, we were astounded at the great number of people and the quantities of merchandise, and at the orderliness and good arrangements that prevailed, for we had never seen such a thing before. The chieftains who accompanied us pointed everything out. Every kind of merchandise was kept separate and had its fixed place marked for it.

Let us begin with the dealers in gold, silver, and precious stones, feathers, cloaks, and embroidered goods, and male and female slaves who are also sold there. They bring as many slaves to be sold in that market as the Portuguese bring Negroes from Guinea. Some are brought there attached to long poles by means of collars round their necks to prevent them from escaping, but others are left loose. Next there were those who sold coarser cloth, and cotton goods and fabrics made of twisted thread, and there were chocolate merchants with their chocolate. In this way you could see every kind of merchandise to be found anywhere in New Spain, laid out in the same way as goods are laid out in my own district of Medina del Campo, a centre for fairs, where each line of stalls has its own particular sort. So it was in this great market. There were those who sold sisal cloth and ropes and the sandals they wear on their feet, which are made from the same plant. All these were kept in one part of the market, in the place assigned to them, and in another part were skins of tigers and lions, otters, jackals, and deer, badgers, mountain cats, and other wild animals, some tanned and some untanned, and other classes of merchandise.

There were sellers of kidney-beans and sage and other vegetables and herbs in another place, and in yet another they were selling fowls, and birds with great dewlaps, also rabbits, hares, deer, young ducks, little dogs, and other such creatures. Then there were the fruiterers; and the women who sold cooked food, flour and honey cake, and tripe, had their part of the market. Then came pottery of all kinds, from big water-jars to little jugs, displayed in its own place, also honey, honey-paste, and other sweets like nougat. Elsewhere they sold timber too, boards, cradles, beams, blocks, and benches, all in a quarter of their own.

Then there were the sellers of pitch-pine for torches, and other things of that kind, and I must also mention, with all apologies, that they sold many canoe-loads of human excrement, which they kept in the creeks near the market. This was for the manufacture of salt and the curing of skins, which they say cannot be done without it. I know that many gentlemen will laugh at this, but I assure them it is true. I may add that on all the roads they have shelters made of reeds or straw or grass so that they can retire when they wish to do so, and purge their bowels unseen by passers-by, and also in order that their excrement shall not be lost.

But why waste so many words on the goods in their great market? If I describe everything in detail I shall never be done. Paper, which in Mexico they call *amal*, and some reeds that smell of liquidamber, and are full of tobacco, and yellow ointments and other such things, are sold in a separate part. Much cochineal is for sale too, under the arcades of that market, and there are many sellers of herbs and other such things. They have a building there also in which three judges sit, and there are officials like constables who examine the merchandise. I am forgetting the sellers of salt and the makers of flint knives, and how they split them off the stone itself, and the fisherwomen and the men who sell small cakes made from a sort of weed which they get out of the great lake, which curdles and forms a kind of bread which tastes rather like cheese. They sell axes too, made of bronze and copper and tin, and gourds and brightly painted wooden jars.

We went on the great *cue*, and as we approached its wide courts, before leaving the market-place itself, we saw many more merchants who, so I was told, brought gold to sell in grains, just as they extract it from the mines. This gold is placed in the thin quills of the large geese of that country, which are so white as to be transparent. They used to reckon their accounts with one another by the length and thickness of these little quills, how much so many cloaks or so many gourds of chocolate or so many slaves were worth, or anything else they were bartering.

Now let us leave the market, having given it a final glance, and come to the courts and enclosures in which their great *cue* stood. Before reaching it you passed through a series of large courts, bigger I think than the Plaza at Salamanca. These courts were surrounded by a double masonry wall and paved, like the whole place, with very large smooth white flagstones. Where these stones were absent everything was whitened and polished, indeed the whole place was so clean that there was not a straw or a grain of dust to be found there.

When we arrived near the great temple and before we had climbed a single step, the great Montezuma sent six *papas* and two chieftains down from the top, where he was making his sacrifices, to escort our Captains; and as he climbed the steps, of which there were one hundred and fourteen, they tried to take him by the arms to help him up in the same way as they helped Montezuma, thinking he might be tired, but he would not let them near him.

The top of the *cue* formed an open square on which stood something like a platform, an it was here that the great stones stood on which they placed the poor Indians for sacrifice. Here also was a massive image like a dragon, and other hideous figures, and a great deal of blood that had been spilled that day. Emerging in the company of two *papas* from the shrine which houses his accursed images, Montezuma made a deep bow to us all and said: 'My lord Malinche, you must be tired after climbing this great *cue* of ours.' And Cortes replied that none of us was ever exhausted by anything. Then Montezuma took him by the hand, and told him to look at his great city and all the other cities standing in the water, and the many others on the land round the lake; and he said that if Cortes had not had a good view of the great market-place he could see it better from where he now was. So we stood there looking, because that huge accursed *cue* stood so high that it dominated everything. We saw the three causeways that led into Mexico: the causeway of Iztapalapa by which we had entered four days before, and that of Tacuba along which we were afterwards to flee on the night of our great defeat, when the new prince Cuitlahuac drove us out of the city (as I shall tell in due course), and that of Tepeaquilla. We saw the fresh water which came from Chapultepec to supply the city, and the bridges that were constructed at intervals on the causeways so that the water could flow in and out from one part of the lake to another. We saw a great number of canoes, some coming with provisions and others returning with cargo and merchandise; and we saw too that one could not pass from one house to another of that great city and the other cities that were built on the water except over wooden drawbridges or by canoe. We saw *cues* and shrines in these cities that looked like gleaming white towers and castles: a marvellous sight. All the houses had flat roofs, and on the causeways were other small towers and shrines built like fortresses.

Having examined and considered all that we had seen, we turned back to the great market and the swarm of people buying and selling. The mere murmur of their voices talking was loud enough to be heard more than three miles away. Some of our soldiers who had been in many parts of the world, in Constantinople, in Rome, and all over Italy, said that they had never seen a market so well laid out, so large, so orderly, and so full of people.

But to return to our Captain, he observed to Father Bartolome de Olmedo, whom I have often mentioned and who happened to be standing near him: 'It would be a good thing, I think, Father, if we were to sound Montezuma as to whether he would let us build a church here.' Father Bartolome answered that it would be a good thing if it were successful, but he did not think this a proper time to speak of it, for Montezuma did not look as if he would allow such a thing.

Cortes, however, addressed Montezuma through Doña Marina: 'Your lordship is a great prince and worthy of even greater things. We have enjoyed the sight of your cities, and since we are now here in your temple, I beg of you to show us your gods and *Teules*.' Montezuma answered that first he would consult his chief *papas*; and when he had spoken to them he said that we might enter a small tower, an apartment like a sort of hall, in which there were two altars with very rich wooden carvings over the roof. On each altar was a giant figure, very tall and very fat. They said that the one on the right was Huichilobos, their war-god. He had a very broad face and huge terrible eyes. And there were so many precious stones, so much gold, so many pearls and seed-pearls stuck to him with a paste which the natives made from a sort of root, that his whole body and head were covered with them. He was girdled with hugh snakes made of gold and precious stones, and in one hand he held a bow, in the other some arrows. Another smaller idol beside him, which they said was his page, carried a short lance and a very rich shield of gold and precious stones. Around Huichilobos' neck hung some Indian faces and other objects in the shape of hearts, the former made of gold and the latter of silver, with many precious blue stones.

There were some smoking braziers of their incense, which they call copal, in which they were burning the hearts of three Indians whom they had sacrificed that day; and all the walls of that shrine were so splashed and caked with blood that they and the floor too were black. Indeed, the whole place stank abominably. We then looked to the left and saw another great image of the same height as Huichilobos, with a face like a bear and eyes that glittered, being made of their mirror-glass, which they call *tezcat*. Its body, like that of Huichilobos, was encrusted with precious stones, for they said that the two were brothers. This Tezcatlipoca, the god of hell, had charge of the Mexicans' souls, and his body was surrounded by figures of little devils with snakes' tails. The walls of this shrine also were so caked with blood and the floor so bathed in it that the stench was worse than that of any slaughter-house in Spain. They had offered that idol five hearts from the day's sacrifices.

At the very top of the *cue* there was another alcove, the woodwork of which was very finely carved, and here there was another image, half man had half lizard, encrusted with precious stones, with half its body covered in a cloak. They said that the body of this creature contained all the seeds in the world, and that he was the god of seedtime and harvest. I do not remember his name. Here too all was covered with blood, both walls and altar, and the stench was such that we could hardly wait to get out. They kept a very large drum there, and when they beat it the sound was most dismal, like some music from the infernal regions, as you might say, and it could be heard six miles away. This drum was said to be covered with skins of huge serpents. In that small platform were many more diabolical objects, trumpets great and small, and large knives, and many hearts that had been burnt with incense before their idols; and everything was caked with blood. The stench here too was like a slaughter-house, and we could scarcely stay in the place.

Our Captain said to Montezuma, through our interpreters, with something like a laugh: 'Lord Montezuma, I cannot imagine how a prince as great and wise as your Majesty can have failed to realize that these idols of yours are not gods but evil things, the proper name for which is devils. But so that I may prove this to you, and make it clear to all your *papas*, grant me one favour. Allow us to erect a cross here on the top of this tower, and let us divide off a part of this sanctuary where your Huichilobos and Tezcatlipoca stand, as a place where we can put an image of Our Lady'—which image Montezuma had already seen—'and then you will see, by the fear that your idols have of her, how grievously they have deceived you.'

Montezuma, however, replied in some temper (and the

two *papas* beside him showed real anger): 'Lord Malinche, if I had known that you were going to utter these insults I should not have shown you my gods. We hold them to be very good. They give us health and rain and crops and weather, and all the victories we desire. So we are bound to worship them and sacrifice to them, and I beg you to say nothing more against them.'

On hearing this and seeing Montezuma's fury, our Captain said no more on the subject but observed cheerfully: 'It is time for your Majesty and ourselves to depart.' Montezuma replied that this was so, but that he had to pray and offer certain sacrifices on account of the great *tatacul*—that is to say sin—which he had committed in allowing us to climb his great *cue* and in being instrumental in letting us see his gods and in the dishonour we had done them by our abuse. Therefore before he left he must pray and worship.

'If that is so, my lord,' Cortes answered, 'I ask your pardon.' And we went down the steps, of which there were a hundred and fourteen, as I said. As some of our soldiers were suffering from pustules or running sores, their thighs pained them as they went down.

I will now give my impression of the *cue*'s surroundings. Do not be surprised, however, if I do not describe them as accurately as I might, for I had other thoughts in my head at the time than that of telling a story. I was more concerned with my military duties and the orders my Captain had given me. But to come to the facts, I think the site of the great *cue* was equal to the plots of six large town houses at home. It tapered from the base to the top of the small tower where they kept their idols. Between the middle of this tall *cue* and its highest point there were five holes like loopholes for cannon, but open and unprotected. But as there are many *cues* painted on the banners of the conquerors, including my own, anyone who has seen them can gather what a *cue* looked like from the outside. I heard a report that, at the time when this great *cue* was built, all the inhabitants of that mighty city placed offerings of gold and silver and pearls and precious stones in the foundations, and bathed them in blood of prisoners of war whom they had sacrificed. They also put there every kind of seed that grew in their country, so that their idols should give them victories and riches and great crops. Some curious readers may ask how we came to know that they had thrown gold and silver and precious *chalchihuites* and seeds into the foundation of the *cue*, and watered them with the blood of Indian victims, seeing that the building was erected a thousand years ago. My answer is that after we conquered that great and strong city and divided the ground we decided to build a church to our patron and guide St James in place of Huichilobos' *cue*, and a great part of the site was taken for the purpose. When the ground was excavated to lay a foundation, gold and silver and *chalchihuites*, and pearls, seed-pearls, and other precious stones were found in great quantities; and a settler in Mexico who built on another part of the site found the same. The officers of His Majesty's Treasury demanded this find as rightfully belonging to the King, and there was a lawsuit about it. I do not remember what the outcome was, only that they asked for information from the *Caciques* and dignitaries of Mexico, and from Guatemoc who was then alive, and they affirmed that all the inhabitants of Mexico had thrown jewels and other things into the foundations, as was recorded in their pictures and records of ancient times. The treasure was therefore preserved for the building of St James's church.

Let me go on to describe the great and splendid courts in front of Huichilobos, on the site where that church now stands, which was called at that time Tlatelolco. I have already said that there were two masonry walls before the entrance to the *cue*, and the court was paved with white stones like flagstones, and all was whitened, burnished and clean. A little apart from the *cue* stood another small tower which was also an idol-house or true hell, for one of its doors was in the shape of a terrible mouth, such as they paint to depict the jaws of hell. This mouth was open and contained great fangs to devour souls. Beside this door were groups of devils and the shapes of serpents, and a little way off was a place of sacrifice, all bloodstained and black with smoke. There were many great pots and jars and pitchers in this house, full of water. For it was here that they cooked the flesh of the wretched Indians who were sacrificed and eaten by the *papas*. Near this place of sacrifice there were many large knives and chopping-blocks like those on which men cut up meat in slaughter-houses; and behind that dreadful house, some distance away, were great piles of brushwood, beside which was a tank of water that was filled and emptied through a pipe from the covered channel that comes into the city from Chapultepec. I always called that building Hell.

Crossing the court you came to another *cue*, where the great Mexican princes were buried. This also contained many idols and was full of blood and smoke. It too had doorways with hellish figures; and beside it was another *cue*, full of skulls and large bones arranged in an orderly pattern, and so numerous that you could not count them however long you looked. The skulls were in one place and the bones in separate piles. Here there were more idols, and in every building or *cue* or shrine were *papas* in long black cloth robes and long hoods.

To proceed, there were other *cues*, a short distance away from that of the skulls, which contained other idols and sacrificial altars decorated with horrible paintings. These idols were said to preside over the marriages of men. But I will waste no more time on the subject of idols. I will only say that all round that great court there were many low houses, used and occupied by the *papas* and other Indians who were in charge of them. On one side of the great *cue* there was another, much bigger pond or tank of very clean water which was solely devoted to the service of Huichilobos and Tezcatlipoca, and the water for this tank was also supplied by covered pipes that came from Chapultepec. Near by were the large buildings of a kind of nunnery where many of the daughters of the inhabitants of Mexico dwelt in retirement until the time of their marriage. Here there were two massive female idols who presided over the marriages of women, and to which they offered sacrifices and feasts in order that they should get good husbands.

I have spent a long time talking about the great *cue* of Tlatelolco and its courts. I will conclude by saying that it was the biggest temple in Mexico, though there were many other fine ones, for every four or five parishes or districts supported a shrine with idols; and since there were many districts I cannot keep a count of them all. I must say, however, that the great *cue* in Cholula was higher than that in Mexico, for it had a hundred and twenty steps. The idol at Cholula, as I heard, had a great reputation, and people made pilgrimages to it from all over New Spain to obtain pardons. This was the reason why they had built it such a magnificent *cue*. It was differently planned from that of Mexico, but also had great courts and a double wall. The *cue* of the city of Texcoco was very high too, having a hundred and seventeen steps, and fine wide courtyards, again of a different shape from the others. Absurd though it was, every province had its own idols, and those of one province or city were of no help in another. Therefore they had infinite numbers of idols and sacrificed to them all.

When we were all tired of walking about and seeing such a diversity of idols and sacrifices, we returned to our quarters, still accompanied by the many *Caciques* and dignitaries whom Montezuma had sent with us.

When our Captain and the Mercedarian friar realized that Montezuma would not allow us to set up a cross at Huichilobos' *cue* or build a church there, it was decided that we should ask his stewards for masons so that we could put up a church in our own quarters. For every time we had said mass since entering the city of Mexico we had had to erect an altar on tables and dismantle it again.

The stewards promised to tell Montezuma of our wishes, and Cortes also sent our interpreters to ask him in person. Montezuma granted our request and ordered that we should be supplied with all the necessary material. We had our church finished in two days, and a cross erected in front of our lodgings, and mass was said there each day until the wine gave out. For as Cortes and some other captains and a friar had been ill during the Tlascalan campaign, there had been a run on the wine that we kept for mass. Still, though it was finished, we still went to church every day and prayed on our knees before the altar and images, firstly because it was our obligation as Christians and a good habit, and secondly so that Montezuma and all his captains should observe us and, seeing us worshipping on our knees before the cross—especially when we intoned the Ave Maria—might be inclined to imitate us.

It being our habit to examine and inquire into everything, when we were all assembled in our lodging and considering which was the best place for an altar, two of our men, one of whom was the carpenter Alonso Yañez, called attention to some marks on one of the walls which showed that there had once been a door, though it had been well plastered up and painted. Now as we had heard that Montezuma kept his father's treasure in this building, we immediately suspected that it must be in this room, which had been closed up only a few days before. Yañez, made the suggestion to Juan Velazquez de Leon and Francisco de Lugo, both relatives of mine, to whom he had attached himself as a servant; and they mentioned the matter to Cortes. So the door was secretly opened, and Cortes went in first with certain captains. When they saw the quantity of golden objects—jewels and plates and ingots—which lay in that chamber they were quite transported. They did not know what to think of such riches. The news soon spread to the other captains and soldiers, and very secretly we all went in to see. The sight of all that wealth dumbfounded me. Being only a youth at the time and never having seen such riches before, I felt certain that there could not be a store like it in the whole world. We unanimously decided that we could not think of touching a particle of it, and that the stones should immediately be replaced in the doorway, which should be blocked again and cemented just as we had found it. We resolved also that not a word should be said about this until times changed, for fear Montezuma might hear of our discovery.

Let us leave this subject of the treasure and tell how four of our most valiant captains took Cortes aside in the church, with a dozen soldiers who were in his trust and confidence, myself among them, and asked him to consider the net or trap in which we were caught, to look at the great strength of the city and observe the causeways and bridges, and remember the warnings we had received in every town we had passed through that Huichilobos had counselled Montezuma to let us into the city and kill us there. We reminded him that the hearts of men are very fickle, especially among the Indians, and begged him not to trust the good will and affection that Montezuma was showing us, because from one hour to another it might change. If he should take it into his head to attack us, we said, the stoppage of our supplies of food and water, or the raising of any of the bridges, would render us helpless. Then, considering the vast army of warriors he possessed, we should be incapable of attacking or defending ourselves. And since all the houses stood in the water, how could our Tlascalan allies come in to help us? We asked him to think over all that we had said, for if we wanted to preserve our lives we must seize Montezuma immediately, without even a day's delay. We pointed out that all the gold Montezuma had given us, and all that we had seen in the treasury of his father Axayacatl, and all the food we ate was turning to poison in our bodies, for we could not sleep by night or day or take any rest while these thoughts were in our minds. If any of our soldiers gave him less drastic advice, we concluded, they would be senseless beasts charmed by the gold and incapable of looking death in the eye.

When he had heard our opinion, Cortes answered: 'Do not imagine, gentlemen, that I am asleep or that I do not share your anxiety. You must have seen that I do. But what strength have we got for so bold a course as to take this great lord in his own palace, surrounded as he is by warriors and guards? What scheme or trick can we devise to prevent him from summoning his soldiers to attack us at once?'

Our captains (Juan Velazquez de Leon, Diego de Ordaz, Gonzalo de Sandoval, and Pedro de Alvarado) replied that Montezuma must be got out of his palace by smooth words and brought to our quarters. Once there, he must be told that he must remain as a prisoner, and that if he called out or made any disturbance he would pay for it with his life. If Cortes was unwilling to take this course at once, they begged him for permission to do it themselves. With two very dangerous alternatives before us, the better and more profitable thing, they said, would be to seize Montezuma rather than wait for him to attack us. Once he did so, what chance would we have? Some of us soldiers also remarked that Montezuma's stewards who brought us food seemed to be growing insolent, and did not serve us as politely as they had at first. Two of our Tlascalan allies had, moreover, secretly observed to Jeronimo de Aguilar that for the last two days the Mexicans had appeared less well disposed to us. We spent a good hour discussing whether or not to take Montezuma prisoner, and how it should be done. But our final advice, that at all costs we should take him prisoner, was approved by our Captain, and we then left the matter till next day. All night we prayed God to direct events in the interests of His holy service.

Next morning two Tlascalan Indians arrived very secretly with letters from Villa Rica containing the news of an attack by the Mexicans at a place called Almeria, in which one of our men and the Constable's horse had been killed, as well as many Totonacs. Moreover the Constable Escalante himself and six more men had died of their wounds after returning to Villa Rica. Now all the hill towns and Cempoala and its dependencies were in revolt. They refused to bring food or serve in the fort; whereas hitherto our men had been respected as *Teules*, now after this disaster Mexicans and Totonacs alike were behaving like wild beasts. They could not control the Indians in any way, and did not know what measures to take.

God knows the distress this news caused us. It was the first defeat we had suffered in New Spain, and misfortunes, as the reader will see, were now descending upon us.

Having decided on the previous day that we would seize Montezuma, we prayed to God all night that His service would profit by the turn of events, and next morning we decided on our course of action.

Cortes took with him five captains, Pedro de Alvarado, Gonzalo de Sandoval, Juan Velazquez de Leon, Francisco de Lugo, Alonso de Avila, and myself, together with Doña Marina and Aguilar. He warned us all to keep very alert, and the horsemen to have their mounts saddled and bridled. I need not say that we were armed, since we went about armed by day and night, with our sandals always on our feet—for at that time we always wore sandals—and Montezuma was used to seeing us like this whenever we went to speak with him. He was neither surprised nor alarmed, therefore, when Cortes and the captains who had come to seize him approached him fully armed.

When we were all prepared, our captains sent to inform the prince that we were coming to his palace. This had always been our practice, and we did not wish to frighten him by making a sudden appearance. Montezuma guessed that the reason for Cortes' visit was his indignation about the attack on Escalante. But although apprehensive, he sent him a message of welcome.

On entering, Cortes made his usual salutations, and said to Montezuma through our interpreters: 'Lord Montezuma, I am greatly astonished that you, a valiant prince who have declared yourself our friend, should have ordered your captains stationed on the coast near Tuxpan to take up arms against my Spaniards. I am astonished also at their boldness in robbing towns which are in the keeping and under the protection of our King and master, and demanding of them Indian men and women for sacrifice, also that they should have killed a Spaniard, who was my brother, and a horse.'

Cortes did not wish to mention Escalante and the six soldiers who had died on reaching Villa Rica, since Montezuma did not know of their deaths, nor did the Indian captains who had attacked them. Therefore he continued: 'Being so much your friend, I ordered my captains to help and serve you in every possible way. But Your Majesty has acted in quite the opposite fashion towards us. In the affray at Cholula your captains and a host of your warriors received your express commands to kill us. Because of my great affection for you I overlooked this at the time. But now your captains and vassals have once more lost all shame and are secretly debating whether you do not again wish to have us killed. I have no desire to start a war on this account, or to destroy this city. Everything will be forgiven, provided you will now come quietly with us to our quarters, and make no protest. You will be as well served and attended there as in your own palace. But if you cry out, or raise any commotion, you will immediately be killed by these captains of mine, whom I have brought for this sole purpose.'

This speech dumbfounded Montezuma. In reply he said that he had never ordered his people to take up arms against us, and that he would at once send to summon his captains so that the truth should be known and they be punished. Thereupon he immediately took the sign and seal of Huichilobos from his wrist, which he never did except when giving some order of the first importance that had to be carried out at once. As to being made a prisoner and leaving his palace against his will, he said that he was not a person to whom such orders could be given, and that it was not his wish to go. Cortes answered him with excellent arguments, which Montezuma countered with even better, to the effect that he refused to leave his palace. More than half an hour passed in these discussions. But when Juan Velazquez de Leon and the other captains saw that time was being wasted, they became impatient to remove Montezuma from his palace and make him a prisoner. Turning to Cortes, Velazquez observed somewhat angrily: 'What is the use of all these words? Either we take him or we knife him. If we do not look after ourselves now we shall be dead men.'

Juan Velazquez spoke in his usual high and terrifying voice; and Montezuma, realizing that our captains were angry, asked Doña Marina what they were saying so loudly, and she, being very quickwitted, replied: 'Lord Montezuma, I advise you to accompany them immediately to their quarters and make no protest. I know they will treat you very honourably as the great prince you are.

But if you stay here, you will be a dead man. In their quarters the truth will be discovered.'

Then Montezuma said to Cortes: 'Lord Mallinche, I see what is in your mind. But I have a son and two legitimate daughters. Take them as hostages and spare me this disgrace. What will my chieftains say if they see me carried off a prisoner?'

Cortes replied that there was no alternative, he must come with us himself; and after a good deal of argument Montezuma agreed to go. Then Cortes and our captains addressed him most ingratiatingly, saying that they begged him humbly not to be angry, and to tell his captains and his guard that he was going of his own free will, since on consulting his idol Huichilobos and the *papas* who served him he had learnt that for the sake of his health and the safety of his life he must stay with us. Then his fine litter was brought, in which he used to go out attended by all his captains, and he was taken to our quarters, where guards and a watch were put over him.

Cortes and the rest of us did our best to provide him with all possible attentions and amusement, and he was put under no restraint. Soon his nephews and all the principal Mexican chieftains visited him to inquire the reasons for his imprisonment, and to ask whether he wished them to make war on us. Montezuma replied that he was spending some days with us of his own free will and under no constraint, that he was happy and would tell them when he wanted anything of them. He told them not to disturb either themselves or the city, and not to be distressed, since his visit was agreeable to Huichilobos, as he had learnt from certain *papas* who had consulted that idol.

This is the way in which the great Montezuma was made prisoner; and there in his lodging he had his servants, his women, and the baths in which he bathed; and twenty good lords, captains, and counsellers remained continuously with him as before. He showed no resentment at being detained. Ambassadors from distant lands came to him where he was, bringing them suits or tribute, and important business was conducted there.

I remember that when important *Caciques* came from far away to discuss boundaries or the ownership of towns or other such business, however great they might be, they would take off their rich robes and put on poor ones of sisal cloth. They had to appear before him barefoot, and on entering his apartments did not pass straight in but up one side. When a *Cacique* came before the great Montezuma he gazed on the ground; and before approaching him he made three bows, saying as he did so: 'Lord, my lord, my great lord!' Then he presented a drawing or painting upon sisal cloth, representing the suit or question upon which he had come, and pointed out the grounds for his claim with a thin polished stick. Beside Montezuma stood two old men, who were great *Caciques*; and when they thoroughly understood the pleadings, these judges told Montezuma the rights of the case, which he then settled in a few words, by which the ownership of the land or villages in question was decided. Thereupon the litigants said no more, but retired without turning their backs, and after making the customary three bows went out into the hall. On leaving Montezuma's presence, they put on other rich robes, and took a walk through the city of Mexico.

Leaving the subject of Montezuma's imprisonment, I will now tell how the messengers whom he sent with his sign and seal to summon the captains who had killed our soldiers brought them before him as prisoners. What he said to them I do not know, but he sent them to Cortes for judgement. Montezuma was not present when their confession was taken, in which they admitted the facts and agreed that their prince had ordered them to wage war, to recover tribute and, should any *Teules* take part in the defence of the towns, to fight and kill them.

When Cortes was shown this confession, he sent to inform Montezuma that he was deeply implicated, and the prince made such excuses as he could. Cortes answered that he himself believed the confession and that, since our King's ordinances prescribed that anyone causing others to be killed, whether they were guilty or innocent, should himself die, Montezuma deserved punishment. But such, he protested, was his affection and concern for Montezuma, that, even if he were guilty, he would rather pay with his own life than allow the prince to forfeit his. Montezuma was alarmed by this message; and without further discussion Cortes sentenced the captains to be burned to death before the royal palace. This sentence was immediately carried out and, to prevent any interference, Cortes had Montezuma put in chains while they were being burned. The prince roared with anger at this indignity, and became even more alarmed than before. After the burning, Cortes went to Montezuma's apartment with five of his captains, and himself removed the chains; and so affectionately did he speak to the prince that his anger soon passed away. For Cortes told him that he looked on him as more than a brother and that though Montezuma was lord and master of so many towns and provinces, yet he, Cortes, would in time, if it were possible, give him domination over even more lands, which he had not been able to conquer and which did not obey him. He said that if Montezuma now wished to go to his palace he would allow him to do so. This he said through our interpreters, and while he was speaking the tears were seen to spring to Montezuma's eyes. The prince replied most courteously that he was grateful for this kindness. But he well knew that Cortes' speech was mere words, and that for the present it would be better for him to remain a prisoner. For his chieftains being numerous, and his nephews and relations coming every day to suggest they should attack us and set him free, there was a danger that once they found him at liberty they would force him to fight us. He did not want to see a rebellion in his city, he said, and feared that if he did not give in to their wishes they might try to set up another prince in his place. So he had put these thoughts out of their heads, he concluded, by informing them that his god Huichilobos had told him he must remain a prisoner. From what we understood, however, there seemed little doubt that Aguilar had said to Montezuma privately, on Cortes' instructions, that though Malinche might order his release the rest of us captains and soldiers would never agree to it.

On hearing this reply, Cortes threw his arms round the prince and embraced him, saying: 'How right I am, Lord Montezuma, to love you as dearly as I love myself!' Then Montezuma asked Cortes that the page called Orteguilla, who already knew the language, might attend him, and this was of great benefit both to him and to us. For from this page, of whom he asked many questions, Montezuma learnt a great deal about Spain, and we learnt what his captains said to him. So useful was Orteguilla to the prince that he became very fond of him.

Montezuma was quite delighted by the great flattery and attention he received and the conversations he had with us all. Whenever we came into his presence, all of us—even Cortes himself—would take off our mailed caps or helmets—for we always went armed—and he treated us with great civility and honour.

Our Captain was very thorough in every way. Fearing that Montezuma might be depressed by his imprisonment, he endeavoured every day after prayers—for we had no wine for mass—to go to pay him court in his captivity. He went accompanied by four captains, and usually Pedro de Alvarado, Juan Velazquez de Leon, and Diego de Ordaz were of that number. They would ask Montezuma most deferentially how he was, and request him to issue his orders, which would be carried out, and beg him not to be distressed by his imprisonment He would reply that, on the contrary, he was glad to be a prisoner, since either our gods gave us power to confine him or Huichilobos permitted it. In one conversation after another they offered him a fuller explanation of the tenets of our holy faith and of the great power of our lord the Emperor.

Then sometimes Montezuma would play Cortes at *totoloque*, a game played with small, very smooth gold pellets specially made for it. They would throw these pellets a considerable distance, and some little slabs as well which were also of gold, and in five throws they either gained or lost certain pieces of gold or rich jewels that they had staked. I remember that Pedro de Alvarado was once keeping the score for Cortes, and one of Montezuma's nephews, a great chief, was doing the same for Montezuma; and Pedro de Alvarado was always marking one point more than Cortes gained. Montezuma saw this and observed with a courteous smile that he did not like Tonatio—which was their name for Pedro de Alvarado—marking, for Cortes, because he made too much *ixoxol* in the score, which means in their language that he cheated by always adding an extra point. We who were on guard at the time could not help laughing at Montezuma's remark, nor could Cortes himself. You may ask why the remark amused us. It was because Pedro de Alvarado, though handsome and good-mannered, had the bad habit of talking too much. Knowing his character so well we were overcome by laughter. But to return to the game. If Cortes won he gave the jewels to those nephews and favourites of Montezuma who attended him, and if Montezuma won he divided them among us soldiers of the guard. In addition to what we gained from the game, he unfailingly gave presents of gold and cloth every day to us and the captain on guard, at that time Juan Velazquez de Leon, who in every way showed himself Montezuma's true friend and servant.

Let us now go on to say that Montezuma told Cortes he wished to go to visit his temple, and make sacrifices, and pay the necessary devotion to his gods. He said that this must be done so that his captains and chiefs might observe it, especially certain nephews of his who came every day to tell him that they wished to free him and make war on us. He answered them that he was glad to stay with us, in the hopes of convincing them that what he had said before was true and his god Huichilobos had really commanded him to stay.

Cortes replied that, as for this request, he must take

care not to do anything that would cost him his life. To prevent any disorders, or any commands to his captains or *papas* to release him to make war on us, he would send captains and soldiers with him who would immediately stab him to death if they detected any change in his bearing. Cortes said that Montezuma was welcome to go, but must not sacrifice any human beings, for this was a great sin against the true God, about whom we had preached to him, and that here were our altars and the image of Our Lady before which he could pray. Montezuma said that he would not sacrifice a single human being, and went off in his grand litter, in his usual great state, accompanied by his *Caciques*. They carried his insignia in front of him, a sort of staff or rod which denoted that his royal person was going that way, and the custom is still followed today by the viceroys of New Spain. With him as guard went four of our captains, Juan Velazquez de Leon, Pedro de Alvarado, Alonso de Avila, and Francisco de Luga, with a hundred and fifty soldiers; and the Mercedarian friar also went with us to stop any attempt at human sacrifice. So we went to the *cue* of Huichilobos; and as we approached that accursed temple, Montezuma ordered them to lift him from his litter. He was then supported on the arms of his nephews and other *Caciques* up to the *cue* itself. As I have already stated, all the chiefs had to keep their eyes downcast while he passed through the streets, and could never look him in the face. When we reached the foot of the steps that lead to the shrine, there were many *papas* waiting to support him as he climbed.

Four Indians had already been sacrificed there the night before and, despite our Captain's protest and the discussions of the Mercedarian friar, Montezuma insisted on killing some more men and boys for his own sacrifice. We could do nothing at the time except pretend to overlook it, for Mexico and the other great cities were on the point of rebelling under Montezuma's nephews, as I shall in due course relate. When Montezuma had completed his sacrifices, which he did very quickly, we returned with him to our quarters. He was very cheerful and gave presents of jewels to us soldiers who had escorted him.

Meanwhile, however, the nephews and kindred of the great Montezuma agreed with other *Caciques* throughout the country that we should be attacked and Montezuma released, and that some of them should proclaim themselves kings of Mexico.

When Cacamatzin, lord of the largest and most important city in New Spain except Mexico, heard that his uncle Montezuma had been imprisoned for some days and that we were taking control in every way we could, and when he got news also that we had opened the chamber where the great treasure of his grandfather Axayacatl was kept, but had so far left it untouched, he decided that before we actually took possession of it something must be done. He called together all the lords of Texcoco, who were his vassals, and the lord of Coyoacan, who was his cousin and Montezuma's nephew, and the lord of Tacuba, and the lord of Iztapalapa, and another great chief who was lord of Matalcingo, a very close relative of Montezuma of whom it was even said that he was the rightful heir to the Caciqueship and kingdom of Mexico. He was a chieftain well known among the Indians for his personal bravery.

While Cacamatzin was arranging with them and other Mexican chieftains that on a given day they should come with all their forces and attack us, it appears that this chief, who was noted for his personal bravery but whose name I cannot remember, said that if Cacamatzin would assure him the kingdom of Mexico, which was rightfully his, he and all his relations, and the chiefs of the province of Matalcingo would be the first to take up arms and either expel us from Mexico or kill us to the last man. Cacamatzin appears, however, to have said that the Caciqueship of Mexico rightfully belonged to him, and that he himself must be king, since he was the nephew of Montezuma, also that if the lord of Matalcingo did not wish to take part he would attack us without him and his people. For Cacamatzin had already won over all the other towns and chiefs I have named, and had arranged the day on which they were to come to Mexico, where they would be admitted by the chieftains of his faction inside the city.

While these negotiations were going on Montezuma learnt all about them from his great relative who was refusing to give in to Cacamatzin's wishes. And to get further information, he sent for all the *Caciques* and chieftains of Texcoco, who told him how Cacamatzin was trying to persuade them all with promises and gifts to help him fight us and release his uncle. As Montezuma was cautious and did not want to see his city rise in armed insurrection, he told Cortes everything that was happening. We and our Captain already knew something about this unrest, but not so much as Montezuma now told us. The advice that Cortes gave him was to give us his Mexican soldiers, and we would then fall on Texcoco and take or destroy both the city and its surroundings. This plan, however, did not suit Montezuma. Cortes then sent a message to Cacamatzin that he must cease his war preparations, which would lead him to destruction, and offered him his friendship, saying that he would do all he could for him and paying him many other compliments.

Now Cacamatzin was a young man and found many others who shared his viewpoint and were eager for war. So he sent Cortes a message, that he understood his flatteries and wished to hear no more from him until they came face to face, when Cortes could say whatever he liked. Cortes then sent Cacamatzin a second message, warning him not to do a disservice to our lord and King, for he would pay for it in person and it would cost him his life. But Cacamatzin relied that he knew no king and wished he had never known Cortes, who by fair words had imprisoned his uncle.

On receiving this answer Cortes implored Montezuma, as he was a great prince, to arrange with the people of Texcoco for Cacamatzin's arrest. For Montezuma had great *Caciques* and kinsmen among his captains in Texcoco who were on bad terms with Cacamatzin and disliked him for his pride. In Mexico itself Montezuma had a young prince in his household, a brother of Cacamatzin and a good-natured lad, who had fled to avoid being killed by him, since he was the next heir to the kingdom of Texcoco. Cortes begged Montezuma either to organize Cacamatzin's arrest with the help of his people in Texcoco, or to send him a secret summons to Mexico and, should he come, to seize him and keep him under restraint until he calmed down. Cortes suggested further that since his other nephew was obedient to him and a member of his household, he should make him lord over Texcoco and take the title away from Cacamatzin, who was working against him and stirring up all the *Caciques* and cities in the land so that he might usurp Montezuma's city and kingdom.

Montezuma promised to send him a summons immediately, and to organize his arrest with his captains and relations should he refuse to come, as he feared he would. Cortes thanked him warmly for this and went so far as to say: 'My lord Montezuma, believe me, you are free to go to your palace if you wish. I see how well disposed you are towards me, and I myself feel great love for you. Were our position not so difficult, indeed, I should not insist on accompanying you, were you and all your nobles to return there. If I have kept you here till now it has been on account of my captains, who contrived your arrest and do not want me to release you, and because Your Majesty says that you prefer to remain in confinement in order to prevent the revolt by which your nephews would attempt to obtain control over your city and deprive you of your authority.'

Montezuma replied by expressing his thanks. But he was getting to understand Cortes' flattering speeches, and saw that his intention was not to release him but to test his good will. Moreover the page Orteguilla had told him that it was really your captains who had advised his arrest, and he must not expect Cortes to release him without their consent. Montezuma said therefore that it would be as well for him to remain a prisoner until he saw what his nephews' plots would lead to, and promised to send messengers to Cacamatzin immediately, asking him to come to Mexico, as he wished to speak to him about making friends with us. As for his imprisonment, he would tell Cacamatzin that he need not worry about it, since had he wanted to free himself many opportunities had been offered, and Malinche had already told him twice that he might return to his palace. However, he did not wish to do so, but to obey the commands of his gods, who had told him that he must remain a prisoner, for if he did not he would soon be dead. This he had learnt some days ago from the priests who ministered to his idols, and for this reason it would be as well to keep friendly with Malinche and his brothers. Montezuma sent the same message to the captains of Texcoco, telling them that he was summoning his nephew to make friends with us, and that they must be careful not to let this youth turn their heads and persuade them to attack us.

Let us return to Cacamatzin, who understood this message perfectly, and held a consultation with his chiefs as to what should be done. Here he began to brag that he would kill us all within four days, and to call his uncle chicken-hearted for not having attacked us when he was advised to do so, as we came down the mountain towards Chalco where he had his troops all posted and everything prepared. Instead of this, he protested, Montezuma had received us into his city in person as if he supposed we had come to confer some benefit on him, and had given us all the gold that had been brought to him as tribute. What was more, we had broken into the treasure-house of his grandfather Axayacatl, and taken Montezuma himself prisoner, and now we were telling him that he must remove the idols of the great Huichilobos so that we could set up our own in their places. Cacamatzin begged his chieftains to help him prevent bad from becoming worse, and to punish these acts and insults. For all that he had described to them they had seen with their own eyes, and they had even seen us burn Montezuma's own captains.

Now, he said, the people had reached the end of their endurance. They must all unite and make war on us.

Cacamatzin promised his hearers then and there that if the lordship of Mexico fell to him he would make them great chieftains, and he gave them many gold jewels as well. He told them also that he had already arranged with his cousins, the lords of Coyoacan and Iztapalapa and Tacuba, and with his other relations, that they should assist him, and there were other chieftains in Mexico itself who would both help him and admit him to the city at any hour he might choose. Some of them could go along the causeways and all the rest across the lake in their pirogues and small canoes, and they would enter the city without opposition. For his uncle was a prisoner, and they need have no fear of us, since, as they well knew, in the affair at Almeria only a few days ago his uncle's captains had killed many *Teules* and a horse, and they had themselves seen the head of the *Teule* and the body of the horse. He said they could finish us all off in an hour, and feast on our bodies till they were full.

They say the captains looked at one another after this speech, and waited for those who usually spoke first at councils of war to begin, and that four or five of them replied by asking how they could possibly go without their lord Montezuma's permission and make war in his own palace and city. First, they said, he must be informed of the proposal. If he consented they would accompany Cacamatzin very gladly indeed; but if he did not they did not wish to act as traitors. It seems that Cacamatzin got angry with these captains and ordered that three of them who had given this reply should be imprisoned. There were other captains present at this debate, however, who were relatives of his, and anxious for trouble, and they promised to support him to the death. So he decided to send his uncle the great Montezuma a message that he ought to be ashamed of himself for commanding him to make friends with men who had done him so much harm and dishonour as to keep him a prisoner, and that such a thing was only possible because we were wizards and had robbed him of his great strength and courage with our witchcraft, or because our gods and the great woman of Castile whom we spoke of as our advocate gave us strength to do what we did. And in this last remark he was not wrong. The long and the short of it was that Cacamatzin was coming, in spite of us and in spite of his uncle, to talk to us and kill us.

When the great Montezuma heard this insolent reply, he was greatly annoyed, and at once sent to summon six of his most trusted captains, to whom he gave his seal, also some golden jewels, ordering them to go to Texcoco immediately and secretly show the seal to certain captains and relations of his who resented Cacamatzin's pride and were on bad terms with him. They were then to arrange for the arrest of Cacamatzin and those in his confidence, and to bring them before him at once. The captains departed and explained Montezuma's orders in

Texcoco, and Cacamatzin, who was extremely unpopular, was arrested in his own palace while discussing war-preparations with his confederates, five of whom were arrested with him.

As Texcoco lies beside the great lake, Montezuma's captains prepared a large pirogue with awnings, put Cacamatzin and the five others aboard, and with a numerous crew of oarsmen rowed them to Mexico. Then, when he had disembarked, they put him on a rich litter befitting his kingly rank, and most respectfully brought him before Montezuma.

It seems that when conversing with his uncle, Cacamatzin was more insolent than ever. Montezuma already knew of the plots he had hatched to make himself lord of Mexico, but learnt further details about them from the other prisoners. If he had been angry with his nephew before, he was now doubly so. So he sent him to our Captain to be kept as a prisoner, and released the other captains.

Cortes went at once to Montezuma's chamber in the palace to thank him for this great favour, and orders were given that the young brother of Cacamatzin, who was in Montezuma's company, should be made king of Texcoco. To solemnize the appointment and win the city's approval, Montezuma summoned the principal chieftains of the whole province before him, and after a long discussion they elected the youth king and lord of that great city. He was afterwards named Don Carlos.

When the *Caciques* and petty kings who were lords of Coyoacan, Iztapalapa, and Tacuba, heard of Cacamatzin's imprisonment, and learnt that the great Montezuma knew of their share in the plot to deprive him of his kingdom in favour of Cacamatzin, they were frightened and ceased to make their customary visits to the palace. Meanwhile Cortes was urging and persuading Montezuma to order their arrest and, at the end of a week, to the considerable relief of ourselves and our Captain, they were all in prison secured to a great chain.

When Cortes heard that these three kinglets were in prison and all the cities peaceful, he reminded Montezuma that before we entered Mexico he had twice sent word that he wished to pay tribute to His Majesty, and that since he now knew how powerful our King was and how many lands paid him tribute as their overlord, and how many kings were his subjects, it would be well for him and all his vassals to offer him their obedience, for it is customary first to offer obedience and then to pay tribute. Montezuma answered that he would call his vassals together and discuss the matter with them, and within ten days all the many princes of that territory assembled. But the *Cacique* who was most closely related to Montezuma did not come. He had, as I have already said, a reputation for great valour, which his bearing, body, limbs, and face confirmed. He was also somewhat rash, and at that time he was at one of his towns called

Tula. It was said that he would succeed to the kingdom of Mexico on Montezuma's death.

On receiving his summons, this prince replied that he would neither come nor pay tribute, for the income from his provinces was not enough for him to live on. This answer infuriated Montezuma, who sent some captains to arrest him. But as he was a great lord and had many relatives, he received warning in advance and retired to his province, where they could not then lay hands on him.

Montezuma's discussion with the *Caciques* of all the territory was attended by none of us except the page Orteguilla. The prince is said to have asked them to reflect how for many years past they had known for certain from their ancestral tradition, set down in their books of records, that men would come from the direction of the sunrise to rule these lands, and that the rule and domination of Mexico would then come to an end. He believed from what his gods had told him that we were these men. The *papas* had consulted Huichilobos about it and offered up sacrifices, but the gods no longer replied as of old. All that Huichilobos vouchsafed to them was that he could only reply as he had done before and they were not to ask him again. They took this to mean that they should offer their obedience to the King of Spain, whose vassals these *Teules* proclaimed themselves to be.

'For the present' Montezuma continued, 'this implies nothing. In the future we will see if we get another reply from our gods, and then we will act accordingly. What I command and implore you to do now is to give some voluntary contribution as a sign of vassalage. Soon I will tell you what is the most suitable course, but now I am being pressed for this tribute by Malinche. I beg therefore that no one will refuse. Remember that during the eighteen years that I have been your prince you have always been most loyal to me, and I have enriched you, extended your lands, and given you power and wealth. At present our gods permit me to be held a prisoner here, and this would not have happened, as I have often told you, except at the command of the great Huichilobos.'

On hearing these arguments, they all replied with many tears and sighs that they would obey, and Montezuma was more tearful than any of them. However, he sent a chieftain to us at once to say that next day they would give their obedience to His Majesty.

Within twenty days all the chieftains whom Montezuma had dispatched to collect the gold tribute returned, and as soon as they arrived Montezuma sent for Cortes and our captains, also for certain of us soldiers whom he knew, because we belonged to his guard, and made us a formal address in words like these:

'I wish you to know, my lord Malinche and my lords Captains and soldiers, that I am indebted to your great King and bear him good will, both for being such a great king, and for having sent from such distant lands to make inquiries about me. But what impresses me most is the thought that he must be the one who is destined to rule over us, as our ancestors have told us and even our gods have indicated in the answers they have given us. Take this gold which has been collected; only haste prevents there being more. What I myself have got ready for the Emperor is the whole of the treasure I received from my father, which is under your hand in your own apartments. I know very well that as soon as you came here you opened the door and inspected it all, and then sealed it up again as it was before. When you send it to him, tell him in your papers and letter: "This is sent by your loyal vassal Montezuma." I will also give you some very precious stones to be sent to him in my name. They are *chalchihuites* and must not be given to anyone else but your great prince, for each one of them is worth two loads of gold. I also wish to send him three blowpipes with their pellet-bags and moulds, since they have such beautiful jewel-work that he will be pleased to see them. And I should also like to give him some of my own possessions, though they are small. For all the gold and jewels I had I have given you at one time or another.'

On hearing this speech we were all amazed at the great Montezuma's goodness and liberality. Doffing our helmets most respectfully, we expressed our deep thanks, and in a most cordial speech Cortes promised that we would write to His Majesty of the magnificence and liberality with which he had given us this gold in his own royal name.

After a further exchange of compliments Montezuma dispatched his stewards to have over all the gold and treasure in the sealed chamber. It took us three days to examine it and remove all the embellishments with which it was decorated; and to help us take it to pieces Montezuma sent us silversmiths from Atzcapotzalco. There was so much of it that after it was broken up it made three heaps of gold weighing over six hundred thousand pesos in all, not counting the silver and many other valuables, or the ingots and slabs of gold, or the grains of gold from the mines. With the help of the Indian goldsmiths from Atzcapoltzalco we began to melt this down into broad bars a little more than two inches across, and no sooner was this done than they brought another present, the one which Montezuma had promised to give for himself. It was marvellous to behold so much gold, and the richness of the jewels he gave us. Some of the *chalchihuites* were so fine that among these *Caciques* they were worth a vast quantity of gold. The three blowpipes and their pellet-moulds, all encrusted with pearls and precious stones, and the feather-pictures of little birds set with mother-of-pearl and even smaller birds, were things of very great value. I will not mention the plumes and feathers and other valuables or I shall never bring my recollections to an end. Let me say that all this gold was stamped with an iron die made by order of Cortes and the King's officers appointed by him in His Majesty's name, and with our general consent, to act until further orders. These were at this time

Gonzalo Mejia, treasurer, and Alonso de Avila, accountant, and the die was the royal coat of arms as it appears on a *real* and the size of a four-*real* piece. The rich jewellery, however, was not stamped, since we did not think it ought to be broken up.

For weighing all these bars of gold and silver and the jewels which were not broken up, we had neither weights nor scales. Cortes and these same officers of the King's treasury thought it would be proper, therefore, to make some iron weights, some as heavy as twenty-five pounds, and others of twelve and a half, two, one and a half, and a pound, also of four ounces and other ounce weights. In this way we could not hope to be very exact, but would not be more than half an ounce out in each weighing.

After the weight was taken the King's officers said that the bars and grains and ingots and jewels, all together, came to more than six hundred thousand pesos, and this did not include the silver and the many other jewels which were not yet valued. Some soldiers said there was more. All that remained to be done was to take out the royal fifth, and then give each captain and soldier his share, preserving their shares for those who had remained at Villa Rica. It seems, however, that Cortes attempted to postpone the division until we had more gold, good weights, and a proper account of the total. But most of us said that the division must be made at once. For we had noticed that when the pieces taken from Montezuma's treasury were broken up there had been much more gold in the piles, and that a third of it was now missing, having been taken away and hidden for the benefit of Cortes, the captains, and the Mercedarian friar. We also saw that the gold was still diminishing. After a good deal of argument what was left was weighed out. It amounted to six hundred thousand pesos without the jewels and bars, and it was agreed that the division would be made next day.

First of all the royal fifth was taken. Then Cortes said that another fifth must be taken for him, a share equal to His Majesty's, which we had promised him in the sand-dunes when we made him Captain-General. After that he said that he had been put to certain expenses in Cuba and that what he had spent on the fleet should be deducted from the pile, and in addition the cost to Diego Velazquez of the ships we had destroyed. We all agreed to this and also to pay the expenses of the advocates we had sent to Spain. Then there were the shares of the seventy settlers who had remained at Villa Rica, and the cost of the horse that died, and of Juan Sedeño's mare, which the Tlascalans had killed with a knife-thrust. Then there were double shares for the Mercedarian friar and the priest Juan Diaz and the captains and those who had brought horses, and the same for the musketeers and crossbowmen, and other trickeries, so that in the end very little was left, so little indeed that many of us soldiers did not want to touch it, and Cortes was left with it all. At that time we could do nothing but hold our tongues; to demand justice in the matter was useless There were other soldiers who took their shares of a hundred pesos and clamoured for the rest. To satisfy them, Cortes secretly gave a bit to one and another as a kind of favour and by means of smooth speeches made them accept the situation.

At that time many of the captains ordered very large golden chains to be made by Montezuma's goldsmiths from Atzcapotzalco, and Cortes too ordered various jewels and a great service of plate. Some soldiers too had laid hands on so much that ingots marked and unmarked and a great variety of jewels were in public circulation. Heavy gambling was always going on with some cards which Pedro Valenciano had manufactured out of drum-skins, and which were as well made and painted as the real thing. Such was the state we were in.

It reached Cortes' ears, however, that many of the soldiers were dissatisfied with their share of the gold and said that the heaps had been robbed, so he decided to make them a speech that was all honeyed words. He said that what he had was for us, and that he did not want his fifth but only the share that came to him as Captain-General, and that if anyone needed anything he would give it to him. He said that the gold we had got so far was only a trifle, and that they could see what great cities there were, and what rich mines, and that we should be lords of them all and very rich and prosperous. He used other arguments too, well couched in the manner of which he was a master. In addition he secretly gave golden jewels to some soldiers and made great promises to others, and he ordered that the food brought by Montezuma's stewards should be divided equally among all the soldiers, receiving no greater share himself than the rest.

Now all men alike covet gold, and the more we have the more we want, and several recognizable pieces were missing from the heaps. At the same time Juan Velazquez de Leon was employing the Atzcapotzalco goldsmiths to make him some large gold chains and pieces of plate for his table. Gonzalo Mejia, the treasurer, privately requested him to deliver this gold to him, since it had not paid the royal fifth and was known to belong to the treasure Montezuma had given us. Juan Velazquez, being Cortes' favourite, refused to give up anything, on the plea that he had not taken any share of what had been collected or anything else, but only what Cortes had given him before the bars were cast.

Gonzalo Mejia answered that what Cortes himself had taken and hidden from his companions was enough, and that as treasurer he demanded all the gold that had not paid the royal fifth. One thing followed another, till both men lost their tempers and drew their swords. Indeed if we had not quickly separated them they would have killed one another, for they were men of great character and brave fighters. As it was they emerged from the battle with two wounds apiece.

When news of this came to Cortes he ordered them both to be put in prison, and each to be attached to a heavy chain. But, as many soldiers reported, he privately told his friend Juan Velazquez that he would only be imprisoned for two days and that Gonzalo Mejia, as treasurer, would be released at once. Cortes arrested them to prove to us that justice would be done and Velazquez imprisoned, even though he was hand in glove with him.

The affair of Gonzalo Mejia was rather more complicated. For the treasurer accused Cortes of having secretly taken much of the missing gold. He said that all the soldiers were complaining to him about it, and asking him why as treasurer he did not demand restitution. But this is a long story and I will not pursue it.

Juan Velazquez was imprisoned in a room not far from Montezuma's apartments. Being a large man and very strong, he dragged the chain after him as he moved about the hall, which made a great noise; and when Montezuma heard it he asked the page Orteguilla who it was that Cortes had bound in chains. The page answered that it was Juan Velazquez, who had once been Montezuma's personal guard—and had now been replaced by Cristobal de Olid. Montezuma then asked the reason, and the page answered, on account of some missing gold.

Later in the day, when Cortes was paying him a visit, Montezuma asked him, after the usual civilities and a little preliminary conversation, why he had imprisoned Juan Velazquez, for he was a good and valiant captain. As I have already said, Montezuma knew us all very well, even to our personal characteristics. Cortes answered him half laughingly that it was because he was a bit touched, by which he meant out of his senses, and because, not having received much gold, he wanted to go to Montezuma's towns and cities and demand it of the *Caciques*. For this reason, and to prevent him from killing anyone, he had been put in prison.

Montezuma begged Cortes to release Juan Velazquez and send him to look for more gold, promising that he would give him some of his own, and Cortes pretended that it went against the grain to release him. But at last he said that he would do so to please Montezuma. I believe he sentenced him to be banished from the camp and sent to Cholula with some of Montezuma's messengers to demand gold. Before this, however, he and Gonzalo Mejia were reconciled. Velazquez returned from his banishment, as I observed, within six days, bringing more gold with him, and I observed also that from that time Gonzalo Mejia and Cortes were no longer good friends. I have recorded this although it is outside my story, to show that, under colour of doing justice and striking fear into all, Cortes was capable of great cunning.

There was never a time when we were not subject to surprises so dangerous that but for God's help they would have cost us our lives. No sooner had we set up the image of Our Lady on the altar, and said mass, than Huichilobos and Tezcatlipoca seem to have spoken to their *papas*, telling them that they intended to leave their country, since they were so ill-treated by the *Tueles*. They said that they did not wish to stay where these figures and the cross had been placed, nor would they stay unless we were killed. This, they said, was their answer, and the *papas* need expect no other, but must convey it to Montezuma and all his captains, so that they might at once attack us and kill us. Their gods also observed that they had seen us break up the gold that was once kept in their honour and forge it into ingots, and warned the Mexicans that not only had we imprisoned five great *Caciques* but were now making ourselves masters of their country. They recited many more of our misdeeds in order to incite their people to war.

Wishing us to hear what his gods had said, Montezuma sent Orteguilla to our Captain with the message that he wished to speak to him on very serious business. The page said that Montezuma was very sad and agitated, and that on the previous night and during much of the day many *papas* and important captains had been with him, holding secret discussions which he could not overhear.

On receiving this message Cortes hurried to the palace where Montezuma was, taking with him Cristobal de Olid, the captain of the guard, and four other captains, also Donña Marina and Jeronimo de Aguilar. All paid great respect to the great Montezuma, who addressed them in these words: 'My lord Malinche and captains, I am indeed distressed at the answer which our *Tueles* have given to our *papas*, to me, and to all my captains. They have commanded us to make war on you and kill you and drive you back across the sea. I have reflected on this command, and think it would be best that you should at once leave this city before you are attacked, and leave no one behind. This, my lord Malinche, you must certainly do, for it is in your own interest. Otherwise you will be killed. Remember that your lives are at stake.'

Cortes and our captains were distressed and even somewhat alarmed; which was not surprising, for the news was so sudden and Montezuma was so insistent that our lives were in the greatest and immediate danger. The matter was clearly urgent. Cortes replied by thanking him for the warning, and saying that at the moment he was troubled by two things: that he had no ships in which to depart, since he had ordered those in which we came to be broken up, and that Montezuma would have to accompany us so that our great Emperor might see him. He begged him as a favour therefore to restrain his *papas* and captains until three ships could be built in the sand-dunes. This course, he argued, would be to their advantage, for if they began a war they would all be killed. And to show that he really meant to build these ships without delay, he asked Montezuma to tell his carpenters to go with two of our soldiers who were expert shipbuilders, and cut wood near the coast.

On hearing Cortes say that he would have to come with us and visit the Emperor, Montezuma was even sadder than before. He said he would let us have the carpenters, and urged Cortes to hurry up and not waste time in talk but get to work. In the meantime he promised to tell his *papas* and captains not to foment disturbances in the city, and to see that Huichilobos was appeased with sacrifices, though not of human lives. After this excited conversation Cortes and our captain took their leave of Montezuma and we were all left in great anxiety wondering when the fighting would begin.

Cortes was anxious to find out the cause of the Mexican revolt. It was quite clear to us that Montezuma was distressed about it. Many of those who had been with Pedro de Alvarado through the critical time said that if the uprising had been desired by Montezuma or started on his advice, or if Montezuma had had any hand in it, they would all have been killed. Montezuma had pacified his people and made them give up the attack.

Pedro de Alvarado's account of events was that the Mexicans had revolted in order to free Montezuma, and at the command of Huichilobos, who was angry because we had placed the image of Our Lady and the cross in his house.

This news greatly distressed Cortes and those of us who heard it. We who were used to campaigning against the Indians knew very well what great hosts they always collected, and that however hard we fought, even with our numbers we should be in great hazard of our lives, and of hunger and hardships, since the city around us was so strong.

Cortes immediately ordered Diego de Ordaz to go with four hundred soldiers, among them most of the crossbowmen and musketeers and some horsemen, to examine the situation described by the wounded soldier, and if he found he could pacify the Indians without fighting or disturbance, to do so. He set out to obey these instructions, but had hardly reached the middle of the street down which he was to march when he was attacked by a great number of Mexican bands, while an equal number shot at him from the roofs. The attack was so fierce that at the first assault eight of our soldiers were killed and all the rest wounded, including Diego de Ordaz himself, who received three wounds. They could not advance a single yard, but had to retreat step by step to their quarters. On the way back another good soldier called Lezcano was killed, after doing valiant deeds with his broadsword.

While many bands were attacking, even more came to our quarters, and discharged so many javelins and slingstones and arrows that in the single attack they wounded forty-six of our men, twelve of whom died of their wounds. So many warriors assailed us that Deigo de Ordaz was unable to retire into our quarters because of the fierce attacks made on him from front and rear and from the rooftops. Our cannon, muskets, crossbows, and lances were of little use; our stout sword-thrusts and our brave fighting were in vain. Though we killed and wounded many of them, they pushed forward over the points of our swords and lances and, closing their ranks, continued to fight as bravely as before. We could not drive them off.

At last, thanks to our cannon, muskets, and crossbows and the damage we did them with our swords, Ordaz was able to enter our quarters. Not till then, hard though he tried, could he force a passage with his badly wounded soldiers, who were reduced by fourteen. Still many bands continued to attack us, crying that we were like women, and calling us rogues and other abusive names, and the damage they had done us till then was as nothing to what was to come. They were so bold that, attacking from different directions, they forced a way into our quarters and set them on fire, and we could not stand up to the smoke and flames till we found the remedy of throwing heaps of earth on top of them and cutting off those rooms from which the fire was coming. Indeed, they believed they would burn us alive in there. These battles lasted all day, and during the night, too, many bands attacked us, hurling javelins, sling-stones, arrows, and stray stones in such numbers that they covered the courtyard and the surrounding ground like corn on a threshing floor.

We spent the night dressing our wounds, repairing the breaches the enemy had made in the walls, and preparing for next day. As soon as dawn broke our Captain decided that we and Narvaez' men combined should sally out and fight them, taking our cannon, muskets, and crossbows, and endeavouring to defeat them, or at least to make them feel our strength and valour better than the day before. I may say that when we were forming this plan the enemy was deciding on similar measures. We fought very well, but they were so strong and had so many bands which relieved one another by turns, that if we had had ten thousand Trojan Hectors and as many Rolands, even then we should not have been able to break through.

I will describe the whole of the battle. We were struck by the tenacity of their fighting, which was beyond description. Neither cannon, muskets, nor crossbows were of any avail, nor hand-to-hand combat, nor the slaughter of thirty or forty of them every time we charged. They still fought on bravely and with more vigour than before. If at times we were gaining a little ground or clearing part of a street, they would pretend to make a retreat, in order to lure us into following them. By thus attacking at less risk, they believed they would prevent us from struggling back alive, for they did us most damage when we were retiring.

Then, as to going out and burning their houses, I have already described the drawbridges between them, which they now raised so that we could only get across through deep water. Then we could not stand up to the rocks and stones which they hurled from the roofs in such numbers that many of our men were hurt or wounded. I do not know why I am writing so calmly, for some three or four soldiers of our company who had served in Italy swore to

God many times that they had never seen such fierce fighting, not even in Christian wars, or against the French king's artillery, or the Great Turk; nor had they ever seen men so courageous as those Indians at charging with closed ranks.

With great difficulty we withdrew to our quarters, hard pressed by many bands of yelling and whistling warriors, who blew their trumpets and beat their drums, calling us rogues and cowards who did not dare to meet them in a day's battle but turned away in flight.

Ten or twelve more soldiers were killed that day, and we all returned badly wounded. We spent the night coming to the decision that in two days' time every able-bodied soldier in the camp would sally forth under the protection of four engines, which we would construct. These were to take the form of strong timber towers, each capable of sheltering twenty-five men, and provided with apertures and loopholes which were to be manned by musketeers and crossbowmen; and close beside them were to march the other soldiers, musketeers and crossbowmen, and the artillery and all the rest; and the horsemen were to make charges.

After settling on this plan, we spent the next day building the machines and strengthening the many breaches they had made in the walls. We did not go out to fight that day. I cannot describe the bands of warriors who came to attack us in our quarters, not just at ten or twelve points but at more than twenty. We were divided among them all, and stationed in many other places too. While we bricked ourselves in and strengthened our fortifications, many other bands openly endeavoured to break into our quarters, and neither guns, crossbows, nor muskets, neither frequent charges nor sword-thrusts, were enough to drive them back. Not one of us, they shouted, would remain alive that day. They would sacrifice our hearts and blood to their gods, and with our legs and arms they would have enough to glut themselves at their feasts. They would throw our bodies for the tigers, lions, vipers, and serpents to gorge on; and for that reason orders had been given that for the last two days the beasts in their cages should be given no food. As for the gold we had, we would get little pleasure from that, or from all our cloth; and as for the Tlascalans who were with us, they would put them into cages to fatten, so that their bodies could be offered one by one as sacrifices. They shouted also, in less violent language, that we must surrender their great lord Montezuma, and they shouted other things as well. At night too, they went on yelling and whistling in the same way, and discharging showers of darts, stones, and arrows.

When dawn broke we commended ourselves to God and sallied forth with our towers. The cannon, muskets, and crossbows went ahead, and the horsemen made charges. But, as I have said, it was to no purpose. Although we killed many of them we could not drive them back. Bravely though they had fought on the previous two days, they were much more vigorous on this occasion and brought up even greater forces. Nevertheless we were determined, even at the cost of our lives, to advance with our towers as far as the great *cue* of Huichilobos.

I will not give a full account of the fighting in one fortified house, or tell how they wounded our horses, which were useless to us. For though they charged the enemy bands, they received so many arrows, darts, and stones that, well-armoured though they were, they could not break the enemy's ranks. If they caught up with any Mexicans, these warriors would quickly jump for safety into the canals or the lake, beside which they had raised fresh walls against the horsemen. There many other Indians were stationed with very long lances to finish them off. If our horses were useless, it was equally useless to turn aside and burn or demolish a house. For, as I have said, they all stood in the water with drawbridges between them. To swim across the gap was very dangerous, for they had so many rocks and stones on their fortified flat roofs that it meant certain destruction to attempt it. In addition to this, when we did set fire to some houses, a single one would take all day to burn, and one did not catch light from the other, because their roofs were flat and because of the water between. It was no good our risking our lives in his direction, therefore, so we made for the great *cue*.

Suddenly more than four thousand warriors ascended it, to reinforce the bands already posted there with long lances and stones and darts. Then all of them together took up a defensive position, and for a long time prevented our ascending the steps. Neither our towers, nor our cannon or crossbows, nor our muskets were of any avail; and although our horsemen tried to charge, the horses lost their foothold and fell down on the great slippery flagstones with which the whole courtyard was paved. While those on the steps of the *cue* prevented our advance, we had so many of the enemy also on both our flanks that although ten or fifteen of them might fall to one cannon-shot, and many others were killed by sword-thrusts and charges, the hosts against us were overwhelming. For a long time we could not ascend the *cue*, although we most persistently pressed home our attacks. We did not take the towers, for they were already destroyed, but in the end we reached the top.

Here Cortes showed himself the brave man he was! The battle was fierce and the fighting intense. It was a memorable sight to see us all streaming with blood and covered with wounds; and some of us were slain. It pleased Our Lord that we should reach the place where the image of Our Lady used to stand, but we did not find it there. It appears, as we afterwards learnt, that the great Montezuma paid devotion to it, and he had ordered it to be kept safe. We set fire to their idols, and a large part of the hall in which Huichilobos and Tezcatlipoca stood was burnt down. In all this we received great help from the Tlascalans. And when we reached the top, some of us fighting and some of us lighting the fire, the *papas* who belonged to that great *cue* were a sight to see! As we retired, however, four or five thousand Indians, every one a leading warrior, tumbled us down the steps, six or ten at a time. Then there were some enemy bands posted on the battlements and in the embrasures of the *cue*, who shot so many darts and arrows at us that we could face neither one group of squadrons nor the other. So we resolved, with much toil and risk of our lives, to return to our quarters. Our towers had been destroyed, all of us were wounded, we had lost sixteen men, and the Indians constantly pressed on our flanks and rear. We captured two of their chief *papas* in this battle, whom Cortes told us to bring back with great care.

The Mexican bands continued to attack our quarters most obstinately and tenaciously all the time we were fighting outside. On our laborious return, indeed, we found as many of the enemy in the fortress as in the force that was pursuing us. They had already demolished some walls to force an entry, but they broke off their attacks when we arrived. Nevertheless during what remained of the day they never ceased to fire darts, stones, and arrows, and during the night they not only fired them but yelled also.

We spent the night dressing the wounded and burying the dead, preparing for going out to fight next day, strengthening and adding parapets to the walls they had pulled down and the breaches they had made, and discussing some method of fighting which would cost us less in dead and wounded. But much though we talked we found no remedy at all.

I must mention the abuse which Narvaez' followers hurled at Cortes. They cursed him and the country, and Diego Velazquez too, who had sent them here when they were peacefully settled in their homes in Cuba. They were quite crazy and uncontrolled.

To return to our story, we came to the conclusion that we must ask for peace, in order that we might retire from Mexico. As soon as it was dawn many more bands of warriors arrived and very effectually surrounded our quarters on every side. The stones and arrows fell even thicker than before, the howls and whistles were even louder, and new bands endeavoured to force an entrance in new places. Cannon and muskets were of no avail, though we did them plenty of damage.

In view of this situation, Cortes decided that the great Montezuma must speak to them from the roof and tell them that the attacks must cease, since we wished to leave the city. When they went to give this message to the prince, it is reported that he said in great grief: 'What more does Malinche want of me? Fate has brought me to such a pass because of him that I do not wish to live or hear his voice again.' He refused to come, and he is even reported to have said that he would not see Cortes again, or listen to any more of his false speeches, promises, and lies. Then the Mercedarian friar and Cristobal de Olid went and talked to him most respectfully and tenderly, and Montezuma answered: 'I do not believe that I can do anything towards ending this war, because they have already chosen another lord, and made up their minds not to let you leave this place alive. I believe therefore that all of you will be killed.'

While the fighting continued, Montezuma was lifted to a battlement of the roof with many of us soldiers guarding him, and began to speak very lovingly to his people, telling them that if they stopped their attacks we would leave Mexico. Many of the Mexican chiefs and captains recognized him and ordered their people to be silent and shoot no more darts, stones, or arrows, and four of them, coming to a place where Montezuma could speak to them and they to him, addressed him in tears: 'Oh lord, our great lord, we are indeed sorry for your misfortune and the disaster that has overtaken you and your family. But we must tell you that we have chosen a kinsman of yours as our new lord.' And they named Cuitlahuac, the lord of Iztapalapa—for it was not Guatemoc, who was lord soon after. They said moreover that the war must be carried on, and that they had promised their idols not to give up until we were all dead. They said they prayed every day to Huichilobos and Tezcatlipoca to keep him free and safe from our power, and that if things ended as they hoped, they would undoubtedly hold him in greater regard as their lord than they had done before. And they begged for his forgiveness.

Barely was this speech finished when a sudden shower of stones and darts descended. Our men who had been shielding Montezuma had momentarily neglected their duty when they saw the attack cease while he spoke to his chiefs. Montezuma was hit by three stones, one on the head, one on the arm, and one on the leg; and though they begged him to have his wounds dressed and eat some food and spoke very kindly to him, he refused. Then quite unexpectedly we were told that he was dead.

Cortes and all of us captains and soldiers wept for him, and there was no one among us that knew him and had dealings with him who did not mourn him as if he were our father, which was not surprising, since he was so good. It was stated that he had reigned for seventeen years, and was the best king they ever had in Mexico, and that he had personally triumphed in three wars against countries he had subjugated.

I have spoken of the sorrow we all felt when we saw that Montezuma was dead. We even blamed the Mercedarian friar for not having persuaded him to become a Christian, but he excused himself by saying that he had not supposed that Montezuma would die of these wounds, though he ought to have ordered them to give him something to deaden the pain. After much discussion Cortes ordered a *papa* and a chief from among our prisoners to go to tell the chief Cuitlahuac and his captains that the great Montezuma was dead, and that they had seen him die, and of the manner of his death and the wounds he had received from his own people. They were to say how grieved we all were, and that they must bury him like the great king that he was, and raise his cousin who was with us to be king in his place, since the inheritance was rightfully his; or else one of his sons, for the prince they had chosen had no right to the succession; and that they should negotiate a peace, so that we could leave the city. Failing that, our messengers were to say that we would sally out to fight them and burn all their houses and do them great damage, since only our respect for Montezuma had prevented us from destroying their city, and he was now dead.

To convince them of Montezuma's death, Cortes ordered six Mexicans, all important men, and the rest of the *papas* whom we held prisoner, to carry him out on their shoulders and hand him over to the Mexican captains, to whom they were to convey Montezuma's orders at the time of his death. For those who carried him out had been present at his deathbed, and they told Cuitlahuac the whole truth, that his own people had killed the prince with three stones.

When they saw Montezuma dead they wept, as we could see, very bitterly, and we clearly heard their shrieks and lamentations. But for all this their fierce attack did not cease; darts, stones, and arrows continued to fly, and they came on again with greater force and fury, crying: 'Now you shall indeed pay for the death of our king and lord, and for your insults to our gods. As for the peace you ask for, come out here and we will settle the terms!'

They said much else that I cannot now remember, about how they had chosen a brave king, who would not be so faint-hearted as to be deceived by false speeches like their good Montezuma. As for his burial, we need not trouble about that, but about our own lives, for in two days not one of us would be left to send them any more messages.

PENGUIN 60s CLASSICS

APOLLONIUS OF RHODES · *Jason and the Argonauts*
ARISTOPHANES · *Lysistrata*
SAINT AUGUSTINE · *Confessions of a Sinner*
JANE AUSTEN · *The History of England*
HONORÉ DE BALZAC · *The Atheist's Mass*
BASHŌ · *Haiku*
GIOVANNI BOCCACCIO · *Ten Tales from the* Decameron
JAMES BOSWELL · *Meeting Dr Johnson*
CHARLOTTE BRONTË · *Mina Laury*
CAO XUEQIN · *The Dream of the Red Chamber*
THOMAS CARLYLE · *On Great Men*
BALDESAR CASTIGLIONE · *Etiquette for Renaissance Gentlemen*
CERVANTES · *The Jealous Extremaduran*
KATE CHOPIN · *The Kiss*
JOSEPH CONRAD · *The Secret Sharer*
DANTE · *The First Three Circles of Hell*
CHARLES DARWIN · *The Galapagos Islands*
THOMAS DE QUINCEY · *The Pleasures and Pains of Opium*
DANIEL DEFOE · *A Visitation of the Plague*
BERNAL DÍAZ · *The Betrayal of Montezuma*
FYODOR DOSTOYEVSKY · *The Gentle Spirit*
FREDERICK DOUGLASS · *The Education of Frederick Douglass*
GEORGE ELIOT · *The Lifted Veil*
GUSTAVE FLAUBERT · *A Simple Heart*
BENJAMIN FRANKLIN · *The Means and Manner of Obtaining Virtue*
EDWARD GIBBON · *Reflections on the Fall of Rome*
CHARLOTTE PERKINS GILMAN · *The Yellow Wallpaper*
GOETHE · *Letters from Italy*
HOMER · *The Rage of Achilles*
HOMER · *The Voyages of Odysseus*

PENGUIN 60s CLASSICS

HENRY JAMES · *The Lesson of the Master*
FRANZ KAFKA · *The Judgement*
THOMAS À KEMPIS · *Counsels on the Spiritual Life*
HEINRICH VON KLEIST · *The Marquise of O—*
LIVY · *Hannibal's Crossing of the Alps*
NICCOLÒ MACHIAVELLI · *The Art of War*
SIR THOMAS MALORY · *The Death of King Arthur*
GUY DE MAUPASSANT · *Boule de Suif*
FRIEDRICH NIETZSCHE · *Zarathustra's Discourses*
OVID · *Orpheus in the Underworld*
PLATO · *Phaedrus*
EDGAR ALLAN POE · *The Murders in the Rue Morgue*
ARTHUR RIMBAUD · *A Season in Hell*
JEAN-JACQUES ROUSSEAU · *Meditations of a Solitary Walker*
ROBERT LOUIS STEVENSON · *Dr Jekyll and Mr Hyde*
TACITUS · *Nero and the Burning of Rome*
HENRY DAVID THOREAU · *Civil Disobedience*
LEO TOLSTOY · *The Death of Ivan Ilyich*
IVAN TURGENEV · *Three Sketches from a Hunter's Album*
MARK TWAIN · *The Man That Corrupted Hadleyburg*
GIORGIO VASARI · *Lives of Three Renaissance Artists*
EDITH WHARTON · *Souls Belated*
WALT WHITMAN · *Song of Myself*
OSCAR WILDE · *The Portrait of Mr W. H.*

ANONYMOUS WORKS

Beowulf and Grendel
Gilgamesh and Enkidu
Tales of Cú Chulaind
Buddha's Teachings
Krishna's Dialogue on the Soul
Two Viking Romances

READ MORE IN PENGUIN